KNITS AT HOME

KNITS AT HOME

RUSTIC DESIGNS FOR THE MODERN NEST

RUTH CROSS

with photography
by Ben Anders

INTERWEAVE.
interweave.com

PUBLISHER Jacqui Small
EDITORIAL MANAGER Kerenza Swift
PROJECT EDITOR Sian Parkhouse
TECHNICAL EDITOR Kristen Ten Dyke
ART DIRECTION & DESIGN Sarah Rock
PRODUCTION Peter Colley

First published in the UK in 2013 by Jacqui Small LLP
an imprint of Aurum Press Ltd
7 Greenland Street
London NW1 0ND

Interweave Press LLC
201 East Fourth Street
Loveland, CO 80537-5655 USA
interweave.com

ISBN 978-1-59668-794-3

CIP data not available at the time of publication

2015 2014 2013
10 9 8 7 6 5 4 3 2 1

Printed in China

CONTENTS

introduction

In a world of shiny surfaces, flat pack furniture, clean lines, and wanting everything done yesterday the craft of hand knitting holds a very special place. Gaining ever more nostalgia as it's passed through the generations, knit remains as strong as ever—a method full of history and yet surprisingly relevant to the contemporary world that has developed alongside it.

Everyone has their own reasons for knitting, but the most unexpected is also one of the most attractive—it takes time. The quietly meditative process of building something with your own hands is a reason in itself to learn, let alone the beautiful things you can create and be truly proud of.

Every hand-knitted piece is made with care, warmth, and character which then radiates from the finished piece in a way so rarely found but so carefully cherished elsewhere in life. Hand knits bring soul to a space.

By combining this craft with clever and considered design, hand knitting will provide both the perfect foil and the perfect complement to contemporary life. I hope you find this book intriguing, challenging, satisfying and enjoyable and I wish you a warm welcome to *Knits at Home*.

Ruth Cross

my inspiration

Knits at Home brings together my love of interiors and my work as a hand-knit designer. I was taught to knit at the age of 21 on a pair of chopsticks while on work placement in New York, left to get on with it, and through trial and error made the rest up. It wasn't until I started working with other knitters that I realized everyone knits differently, but because each of us is individually taught we all assume we do it the same way.

Before learning myself, I thought hand knitting was a waste of time that could only create something old fashioned or kitsch — I couldn't have been more wrong. As a craft it is incredibly undeveloped and yet its capabilities are endless. This, combined with an extremely personal and satisfying process that anyone can try, makes knitting totally fascinating.

One of my main aims for *Knits at Home* is to explain how knit works as a structure and to encourage experimentation around this. Although I've now learned how to write a pattern, I've never actually followed one—I find them too definite in their instruction, leaving little room or allowance for an individual's taste and needs. The patterns I've included in *Knits at Home* are intended to be adaptable; rather than creating a perfect copy of the example, I hope you'll be inspired to create something unique, something that is perfect for you and your home.

The role of individual design and creativity has always been extremely important to me. With hand knitting you invest so much time and care in each piece, it is important that it actually works with and complements your home. Ideally I hope to inspire you to create something that stands up as a piece of design in its own right, which you love all the more for it. My mantra is for hand-knitted designs to look hand made, not home made.

To develop my own designs I find inspiration in all kinds of surprising places, absorbing anything I find interesting, from plants to architecture to music and food and just about anything in between. It doesn't matter what it is, as long as you like it. Half the skill of design is the ability to really look at things and analyze why you like what you like — is it the shape, a detail, color, or texture or something else entirely? You can then bring these elements to your creations, making them richer and more successful. By bringing together inspiration with your own sketches and design ideas you'll be able to visualize your different options before you start — dramatically increasing your chance of making something you love when it's finished! Eventually you'll see a pattern develop within your work, and then realize that you have found your own style.

So, all in all, after years of hand knitting everything under the sun, my hope is that *Knits at Home* helps break the myth of the "right" way to knit, and that it opens the door to some exciting and contemporary development of this ancient craft. Don't listen to anyone who tells you what to do, just have a go and have fun doing whatever works for you.

Happy knitting!

To get started you need some needles and yarn. Needles come in a range of sizes, but to begin pick some that aren't too small or too big to handle. I learned on US 10 (6mm), which is good and remains my favorite today. What you prefer your needles to be made from is something you'll find out for yourself when you've tried a few. I like metal ones with short tapered points (I find long tapers will make your knitting tighter and less easy to play with), but there are also wood and plastic needles available.

BASIC KNITTING

For your first yarn try to pick something chunky and smooth in a light color, which will make your knitting easy to control. (Steer away from the novelty yarns.) On balls of yarn there is a specified needle size written on the label. Don't worry too much about this—it's an indication only. Thrift stores are good places to pick up needles and yarns without spending a fortune. Then, when you've worked out what you like, find your local wool shop for more specific requirements—they will also provide a wealth of knowledge and may even run a knitting group you can join.

Using the instructions on pages 130–131 master the art of casting on, then try knitting and purling whole rows. You need about 20 stitches to give yourself a good-sized piece to practice on. Too few stitches and you'll have nothing to hold; too many and you'll be swamped. The instructions I've given are how I personally knit and purl. Everyone knits slightly differently, but I find this method allows me to play around with the stitches themselves more easily. If you knit differently then the simpler patterns in this book will work just fine, but for the more textural ones you will need to follow my method for a good result.

stripy lavender bags

Endless combinations of knit and purl rows exist (see the next pages for a sampling), but if you're not sure where to start then don't worry—you can dip your toe into the world of knitting with this simple project and soon enough you'll have created your first ever knit.

What you need

- size US 10 (6mm) needles
- a ball of Debbie Bliss Rialto Chunky
- cotton fabric for lining
- dried lavender

What you do

Knit two to make the front and the back

Cast on 18 sts

Rows 1 and 2 purl

Row 3 knit

Rows 4 and 5 purl

Rows 6–9 repeat Rows 2–5

Row 10 knit

Row 11 purl

Rows 12–14 knit

Row 15 purl

Row 16 knit

Row 17 purl

Rows 18–25 repeat Rows 2–9

Bind off knitwise

Sew up 3 of the sides. Cut your lining fabric into 2 squares ¾" (2cm) across bigger than the bag. Sew these together on 3 sides, turn through, and fill with lavender. Sew up the final side and put this into your knitted bag, sew up the fourth side, and sew on a hanging loop.

Simple stripes

When you feel confident knitting and purling a whole row then you can start to play around. By changing the order of your knit and purl rows you will be able to create a whole range of stripes. If you simply alternate between knit and purl you'll get a flat jersey fabric—any other combination will instantly add stripes. When you are playing with the texture like this its important to remember that fabric is double sided. Sometimes what you originally intend as the back looks better than the front so always remember to check—you may need to turn the whole piece over.

This collection of lavender bags was made from squares of the stripes we came up with, so cast on a few stitches, try a few rows and experiment . . .

super easy bedthrow/blanket/scarf

This simple pattern uses big wool and needles to create a very chic effect—there are three widths depending on whether you want a scarf, a blanket, or a full bedthrow. Which version and color you choose is entirely up to you.

What you need

- size US 15 (10mm) needles
- Rowan Big Wool (*we used color 1*) Scarf requires approximately 4 balls. Blanket requires approximately 15 balls. Bedthrow requires approximately 40 balls.

What you do

Cast on 21sts for a scarf, 78ss for a blanket or 208sts for a bedsthrow

This pattern uses slipped stitches (or sl) at the beginning of every row to give a neat raw edge (see page 134)

Row 1 purl
Row 2 sl1 wyif, purl to end
Row 3 sl1 wyib, knit to end
Rows 4 – 9 repeat Rows 2–3
Rows 10 – 49 sl1 wyib, knit every row
Row 50 sl1 wyib, knit to last st, p1
Row 51 sl1 wyif, purl to last st, k1
Row 52 sl1 wyib, knit to last st, p1
Row 53 sl1 wyib, knit to end
Row 54 sl1 wyif, purl to end
Row 55 sl1 wyib, knit to end

Rows 56 – 91 repeat Rows 50 – 55
Row 92 sl1 wyib, knit to last st, p1
Row 93 sl1 wyif, purl to last st, k1
Row 94 sl1 wyib, knit to last st, p1
Row 95 sl1 wyif, purl to last st, k1
Row 96 sl1 wyib, knit to last st, p1
Rows 97 sl1 wyib, knit to end
Row 98 sl1 wyif, purl to end
Row 99 sl1 wyib, knit to end
Row 100 sl1 wyif, purl to end
Row 101 sl1 wyib, knit to end
Rows 102 – 141 repeat Rows 92 – 101
Rows 142 – 146 repeat Rows 92 – 96
Rows 147 – 164 odd rows: sl1 wyib, knit; even rows: sl1 wyif, purl.
Rows 165 – 183 odd rows: sl1 wyif, purl to last st, k1; even rows: sl 1 wyib, knit to last st, p1
Rows 184 – 201 odd rows: sl1 wyib, knit; even rows: sl1 wyif, purl.
Rows 202 – 256 repeat Rows 92 – 146
Rows 257 – 298 repeat Rows 53–55, 50 – 52
Rows 299 – 338 sl1 wyib, knit every row
Row 339 sl1 wyib, knit to end

Row 340 sl1 wyif, purl to end
Row 341–346 repeat Rows 339–340
Bind off purlwise

Scarf 7¾" (20cm) wide
Blanket 29½" (75cm) wide
Bedthrow 78¾" (200cm) wide

All three should measure about 79¾" (200cm) long.

For instructions on how to add fringe see page 110.

KNITTING REALLY WIDE THINGS

The best way to knit really wide things is to use circular needles. Use them exactly like normal needles and then the weight isn't taken by your wrists and a huge number of stitches aren't squashed onto your needles. It's also easier to measure your knitting as you go along. A great tip for new pairs from one of my knitters is to dip the middle section into very hot water then pull it out straight to uncurl the the ends—it works.

Even the simplest knit can have a striking effect on a big scale—the warmth this blanket brings to such a clean room adds an unmissable air of invitation. You can find instructions to knit the Apple Pie Pillow on pages 56–61

Introducing design

Knitting is like baking – once you've mastered the basic knit and purl stitches you can start to play around with each element of the process separately. The easiest way to experiment is simply by changing the yarn. There are no limits as to what can be considered yarn - if it's flexible and in a strip then you can knit with it. It's certainly not just wool out there.

These swatches follow exactly the same instructions but use different yarns and needle sizes so you can see how dramatic the effect can be.

Exploring yarn

To experiment with different materials cast on a number of stitches then switch between yarns to see what happens. Simply tie your new yarn onto the old one at the end of a row and start using it. Don't worry about all the loose ends at the moment. If you keep the needle size and number of stitches the same it will remain a similar width. Don't be too hard on yourself – just try, try, try and evaluate the results. It doesn't have to be beautiful – it's just research for yourself!

When you have found a particular stripe or combination you like, make a note of how you did it then you can work out the gauge (see page 138) and use it to make a pattern for a straight-sided vase (see next page).

vase covers

One of my favorite ways to show off a piece of knitting is to hold it in front of the light, which exposes the structure perfectly. Making vase covers does this brilliantly and pushes knit away from its traditional cozy image to become something truly contemporary.

My readymade vase cover pattern

The vase cover shown far left in the picture opposite uses a combination of purls and knit stitches so is a good way to start.

What you need

- 7mm needles (no exact US equivalent: between US sizes 10.5 and 11 needles). Adjust needle size if necessary to obtain the correct gauge
- a ball of Rowan Big Wool
- a ball of Rowan British Sheep Breeds DK
- a 19" (48.5cm) circumference, 10½" (26.5cm) vase

What you do

Using 2 strands of the DK cast on 58sts

Row 1 purl
Row 2 purl
Drop your strands of DK and pick up 1 strand of Big Wool
Row 3 purl

Row 4 purl
Row 5 knit
Row 6 purl
Change to 2 strands of DK
Row 7 purl
Row 8 purl
Change to 1 strand of Big Wool
Row 9 purl
Row 10 purl
Change to 1 strand of DK
Row 11 purl
Row 12 purl
Change to 1 strand of Big Wool
Row 13 purl
Row 14 purl
Change to 2 strands of DK
Row 15 purl
Row 16 purl
Rows 17–30 repeat Rows 3–16
Change to 1 strand of Big Wool
Row 31 purl
Row 32 bind off knitwise

The wide stripe's flatter, knitted side is the right side so fold wrong sides together and sew up the side. You can then pull it onto your glass vase.

Making a vase cover with your own design

When you've created a stripe you like, you can make your own bespoke vase cover as I did for the vases shown opposite and on the next pages, the result of playing around with the different yarns and stitches found in this book.

First take your vase and measure the circumference. Multiply this by your chosen stripe's stitch gauge (see page 138 to work this out). For instance a 8¾" (22.5cm) circumference vase = 8¾" x 5 sts/in = 44 sts.

To make this cling to the vase deduct 10 per cent of the stitches (so from 44 sts required cast on only 40 sts). Follow your own knit stripe instructions until you've got a long enough piece and bind off when you want. If you use circular needles you can literally hold the piece around the vase and see how it looks as you go along. When you are ready sew up the side seam and pull the cover onto your vase.

Something from nothing

With any luck you've been experimenting like crazy and now have numerous squares of knitting absolutely everywhere. These are perfect to make into a patchwork cushion (or if you've been really productive you could try a blanket!). All you have to do is arrange your pieces into a pattern you like and stitch them together!

IT'S ALL IN THE FINISHING . . . THE ART OF SEWING, WASHING, AND STEAMING

When you've got the hang of knitting you'll soon need to do some finishing. Finishing is everything you need to do after you've knitted the pieces required. Getting finishing right makes all the difference. There must be a million different techniques but my instructions are on page 140. If you follow these instructions your pieces should end up looking lovely!

patchwork pillow cover

This pillow cover is constructed using all the left over pieces from many of the other projects in the book. Each panel is different and you can see from the phot opposite which goes where—obviously you can see what you have on hand and substitute what you have available for anything we have used. If you have any trial pieces that are the right size, you can always use these too. (Some of the techniques used in these panels are covered later in the book so you might want to come back to this project if you're not confident enough just yet.)

What you need
- yarn and needles as indicated
- a 20" (50cm)-square pillow form
- 3 large buttons

What you do
Piece 1 (bottom left)
Stitch gauge $4\frac{3}{4}$ sts/in
Using dark brown (shade 10) Patons Wool Blend Aran and size US 7 (4.5mm) needles cast on 19 sts.
Row 1 purl
Row 2 purl
Row 3 knit
Repeat Rows 2 & 3 until you have a piece about 4" (10cm) wide x 12" (30cm) long. On the next purl row bind off knitwise.

Piece 2 (top right)
Stitch gauge $7\frac{1}{8}$ sts/in
Using gray (shade 92) Patons Merino DK and size US 6 (4mm) needles cast on 57 sts. See page 130 for instructions on KB and PB.

Row 1 purl
Row 2 purl
Row 3 k1 KB x31, k2
Row 4 p1 PB x31, p2
Continue repeating Rows 3 – 4 until your piece is about 8" (20cm) wide x 8" (20cm) long. Bind off knitwise.

Piece 3 (bottom second from right)
Stitch gauge $3\frac{3}{4}$ sts/in
Using cream Debbie Bliss Rialto Chunky and size US $10\frac{1}{2}$ (6.5mm) needles cast on 15 sts.
Rows 1 – 63 purl
Bind off purlwise. This piece should measure about 4" (10cm) wide x 12" (30cm) long.

Piece 4 (bottom right)
Stitch gauge $3\frac{3}{4}$ sts/in
Using blue Debbie Bliss Rialto Chunky and size US $10\frac{1}{2}$ (6.5mm) needles cast on 15 sts.
Row 1 purl
Row 2 purl

Row 3 knit
Repeat Rows 2 – 3 until you have a piece about 4" (10cm) wide x 12" (30cm) long. On the next purl row bind off knitwise.

Piece 5 (top left)
Stitch gauge $5\frac{1}{2}$ sts/in
Using Rowan British Sheep Breeds DK undyed and size US 6 (4mm) needles cast on 44 sts.
Row 1 (k2 p2) x 11
Row 2 p1 (k2 p2) x10, k2 p1
Repeat Rows 1 – 2 until your piece is about 8" (20cm) wide x 12" (30cm) long. Bind off knitwise.

Piece 6 (bottom center)
Stitch gauge $4\frac{3}{4}$ sts/in
Using marled dark blue Patons Wool Blend Aran and size US 7 (4.5mm) needles cast on 38 sts.
Every row purl—continue until your piece is about 8" (20cm) long x 8" (20cm) wide when pulled slightly.

Pieces 7 and 8 (center)

Stitch gauge 3¼ sts/in

Using black/white Rowan Big Wool (one piece in each color) and 7mm needles cast on 13 sts. (No exact US equivalent: between US sizes 10.5 and 11 needles). Adjust needle size if necessary to obtain the correct gauge.

Row 1 knit

Row 2 purl

Rows 3 – 16 repeat Rows 1 – 2

Bind off knitwise. Each piece should measure about 4" (10cm) x 4" (10cm).

When you've made all the pieces arrange them in the right order and sew them together. You can then either use the following pillow back pattern or simply sew a fabric back on — it's entirely up to you.

Back underlap

Stitch gauge 3¾ sts/in

Using gray Debbie Bliss Rialto Chunky and size US 10½ (6.5mm) needles cast on 54 sts.

Row 1 purl

Row 2 sl1 wyif, purl to end

Row 3 sl1 wyib, knit to end

Rows 4 – 101 repeat Rows 2 – 3

Bind off knitwise. This piece should measure about 14¼" (36cm) wide x 19" (48cm) long.

Back overlap

Stitch gauge 3¾ sts/in

Using grey Debbie Bliss Rialto Chunky and size US 10½ (6.5mm) needles cast on 36 sts.

Row 1 purl

Row 2 sl1 wyif, purl to end

Row 3 sl1 wyib, knit to end

Rows 4 – 101 repeat Rows 2 – 3 *

*On Row 21, Row 51 and Row 81 make a 6st buttonhole 3 sts in from edge (see page 138 for instructions)

Bind off knitwise. This piece should measure about 9½" (24cm) wide x 19" (48cm) long.

To sew up see page 139. Sew buttons to underlap, aligning with buttonholes.

For the pattern for the patchwork blanket (shown right) see pages 74-6.

The lovely thing about knitting is that, in its most basic form, it is really simple to do, yet it is easily altered to create endless new designs. By actually playing with the structure of knit a whole new world opens and allows us to create truly exceptional work—nowhere is this more obvious than with the wonderful textures possible. Hand knitting is the only method of making textiles that is so controllable in this way, and that's why we love it. However, when there are no limits, it can be a bit daunting, so I'm going to explain how to create texture one step at a time.

CREATING TEXTURE

So far all our stripes have been horizontal with whole rows of purl or knit. By using knit and purl in the same row we can create clever patterns—the most familiar being the rib, commonly used on cuffs.

A basic rib that will get you started is as follows: cast on a multiple of 4 stitches + 2. Row 1 (k2 p2) repeat to last 2 stitches, k2. Row 2 (p2 k2) repeat to last 2 stitches, p2.

Try altering your yarn and needle size to understand how ribs behave, then try altering the number of purl and knit stitches. Well-constructed ribs can be impressive and are often elastic enough to be used to wrap around shapes without any need to change the number of stitches.

ribbed fruit bowl cover

Ribs in their simplest form can be very effective. Just look at how they work with these chunky wooden fruit bowls, transforming them with a surprising new look.

What you need

- 7mm needles (no exact US equivalent: between US sizes 10.5 and 11) Adjust needle size if necessary to obtain the correct gauge
- a wooden bowl
- a chunky yarn (*we used Rowan Felted Tweed Chunky in color 282 blue and 283 gray*)

What you do

Measure the widest circumference of your bowl and allow 2½ sts per 1". Cast on this many stitches and start with a rib of 2 purls then 2 knits. If your total number of stitches isn't divisible by 4 then just knit/purl what you can for the last repeat. When you do the next row just follow the row below.

To work out how many rows you need for this section measure where you want the cover to start on the base of the bowl to where the widest part is. (Start just in from where the side starts — if your bowl is fairly flat like ours most of the base will not be covered.) Work as many rows as you need to get this length. At this point change to a 3 purls, 3 knits rib (if your row isn't divisible by 6 then do as for the first rib and cut the last repeat short). Work as many rows as you need to reach the top of the bowl, then bind off tightly.

Sew up the side seam and pull the cover over the bowl top first. The rib will spring in to wrap around the bowl's base, but to make sure it stays put we used a long piece of the yarn and went through each stitch of the cast on and pulled it closed to make the cover snug. The firm bind-off edge should be slightly smaller than the bowl's lip and will hold on to this edge — if it is a bit baggy just sew a similar drawstring thread around the top too.

There isn't any limit to what shape these covers can be made for — just use the 2 x 2 rib where you need a tighter spring and a larger rib for a more relaxed fabric.

combining knits and purls for texture

Try combining knits and purls in any order to discover patterns for yourself. As you can see from the table runner on pages 40–43, knitting (essentially a grid) lends itself to checks and stripes, but if you can find diagonal patterns they can be even more effective.

Cast on a few stitches and get started, changing and adapting your ideas as you go (sometimes sketching ideas before can help). However, be careful to give each possible pattern enough stitches and rows to see how it works on a big scale—sometimes patterns just need some consistent repetition to reveal themselves.

Three simple knit/purl stitch patterns to try

Simply repeat the stitches indicated within (parenthesis) as instructed

Fake basket weave

Cast on a multiple of 6 + 1
Row 1 (p1 k2) to last st, p1
Row 2 k1 (p2 k1) to end
Row 3 (p4 k2) to last st, p1
Row 4 k1 (p2 k4) to end
Rows 5 and 6 as Rows 1 and 2
Row 7 p1 (k2 p4) to end
Row 8 (k4 p2) to last st, k1
Repeat Rows 1–8

Mistake stitch rib

Cast on a multiple of 4 + 3
There is only one instruction to this stitch:
(k2 p2) to last 3 st, k2 p1—do every row like this!

Texture diamonds

Cast on a multiple of 8 + 3
Row 1 k1 (p2 k5 p1) to last 2 sts, p1 k1
Row 2 p2 (k2 p3 k2 p1) to last st, p1
Row 3 k3 (p2 k1 p2 k3) to end
Row 4 p4 (k3 p5) to last 7 sts, k3 p4
Row 5 k4 p3 (k5 p3) to last 4 sts, k4
Row 6 p3 (k2 p1 k2 p3) to end
Row 7 k2 (p2 k3 p2 k1) k1
Row 8 p1 (k2 p5 k1) to last 2 sts, k1 p1
Repeat Rows 1–8

adaptable table runner

Combining knits and purls is a simple way to build up a larger-scale pattern. By introducing simple details, as this runner has, we can create something remarkably chic looking.

HOW TO USE REPEATS (USING THIS RUNNER AS AN EXAMPLE)

Measure how long you would like your piece to be. Using the repeat measurements, you can work out what you need as follows:

Take the width of knitting you would like, subtract the width of the additional edge stitches, then divide the rest by the width of one repeat. This will tell you how many repeats and stitches you need. This sum almost never works out exactly, so depending on the look you want you can adjust the size by rounding up/down the amount you cast on.

Each repeat (using the yarn and needles specified) is 22 sts /approx 4" (10cm) wide x 30 rows/ approx 4⅓" (11cm) long. Onto this you need to add 9 additional stitches for the edges of the width (+1¾" [4.5cm]) and 3 rows (+½" [1.3cm]) for the start and end of the piece. Of course if you like the pattern but want it in a different yarn you can just do a few repeats as a stitch sample and use the measurements you take from it.

What you need
- size US 6 (4mm) needles
- Debbie Bliss Amalfi yarn (*we used 10 balls of color 011*)
- ¾" (2mm) wide ribbon, ideally viscose (*we used 94 yds (86m) not including the fringing*)

the quantity needed depends on the size of the piece you make and the ribbon is optional—you could use a contrasting color yarn or ignore this detail completely.

What you do
Cast on (using the ribbon) a multiple of 22 sts + 9. (*We cast on 75 sts or 3 repeats*).

The 22-st repeat section is shown in [brackets], the pattern repeats within this are shown in (parenthesis).

Row 1 purl

Change to the Amalfi yarn

Row 2 sl1 wyif, p1 [p12 k3 p7] x3, p7

Row 3 sl1 wyib, k1 [(k1 p1) x6, p3 (p1 k1) x3, p1] x3, (k1 p1) x2 k3

Row 4 as Row 2

Row 5 sl1 wyib, k1 [(p1 k1) x6, p3 (k1 p1) x3, k1] x3, p1 (k1 p1) x2, k2

Row 6 as Row 2

Row 7 as Row 3

Row 8 as Row 2

Row 9 sl1 wyib, k1 [(p1 k1) x2, p1 k7 p3 k7] x3, (p1 k1) x2, p1 k2

Row 10 as Row 2

Row 11 sl1 wyib, k1 [(k1 p1) x2, k8 p3 k7]) x3, (k1 p1) x2, k3

Row 12 as Row 2

Row 13 as Row 9

Row 14 as Row 2

Row 15 as Row 11

Row 16 as Row 2

Row 17 sl1 wyib, k1, purl to last 2 stitches k2

Row 18 sl1 wyif, p1, knit to last 2 stitches p2

Row 19 as Row 17

Row 20 as Row 2

continued on next page

Row 21 as Row 11
Row 22 as Row 2
Row 23 as Row 9
Row 24 as Row 2
Row 25 as Row 11
Row 26 as Row 2
Row 27 as Row 9
Row 28 as Row 2
Row 29 as Row 3
Row 30 as Row 2
Row 31 as Row 5
Change to ribbon
Row 32 as Row 2
Row 33 as Row 3
Change to Amalfi yarn
Row 34 as Row 2
Row 35 as Row 5
Row 36 as Row 2
Row 37 as Row 3

Rows 8–37 are one repeat
lengthways. Do as many of these
as you need. We did 23 repeats
lengthways. Then to finish repeat
rows 8–33 only and on your next
row bind off using the ribbon. The
runner measures 104.5" (265.5cm)
long x 13¾" (35cm) wide.

We then used the same ribbon to
add a fringe on the ends — see the
embellishment section (page 110)
for help with this.

Everything so far in this book should be taken as a guide —don't think for a second there are actually any set rules to knitting (beyond making sure the basic structure holds together). By now you'll understand that knitting is just a chain that links horizontally and vertically. As long as each stitch of the chain is secure you can start to challenge the basics. The most interesting ideas will come out of not being afraid to experiment and always asking yourself "what happens if . . . ?" Just remember that almost anything in repetition will look good!

MANIPULATING STITCHES

I first started to "manipulate" stitches when I realized how much there was to explore within the structure. Taking inspiration from an interesting texture, I begin to plan how to knit something similar. If it's an uneven look you want, try to be messy—change needles or yarns randomly or work the same stitches several times to create textural bumps. You can intentionally start ladders, sew pieces together or add knitting to other things by hooking them onto your needle like stitches. On the other hand you can be precise and develop a clean, sleek finished cloth. To get started don't worry too much about what it looks like. Just dive in—who knows what you will discover?

introducing new techniques

Below are a few new things to try and some simple patterns for each technique, shown in the samples opposite (clockwise from top left) and in some of the pillows on pages 48–49.

Basket Stitches

One of my favorite techniques is the basket stitch. I'm sure it has many other names but this is what I know it as. See page 130 for instructions on KB and PB.

Cast on an odd number of stitches, knit a row or two then repeat these two rows

Row 1 (KB) to last stitch k1
Row 2 (PB) to last stitch p1

Extra long stitches

To create an open section in your knitting try wrapping the yarn around the needle more than once before you pull through the new stitch. The extra wrap will stay on your needle until the next row when you work it as normal and the long stitch will unwrap itself. You can wrap as many times as you like, as often as you like — there are limitless combinations but here is a simple one to try first:

Cast on any number of stitches
Row 1 purl
Row 2 double length purl
(to get double length wrap the yarn around twice before pulling the purl stitch through)
Repeat these rows
(used in pillow far left page 48)

Lace holes

Lace holes are created by doing a combination of togs and yos (see pages 135 and 136). If you do these actions next to each other you make a neat hole. If you do some normal stitches between the actions you'll get the illusion of whole sections of stitches moving diagonally.

A basic example is as follows:
Cast on a multiple of 12 sts + 1
Row 1 knit
Row 2 p1 (p2tog p9 YO k1)
Repeat Rows 1–2
(a similar pattern is used in the far right pillow on page 49. Once you get the idea, try a variation of decrease stitches paired with the yos and use a different number of plain stitches between them. Have some fun with it.)

Cables

Whole books are written about this simple yet effective technique, known for looking really impressive. See page 137 for the theory of knitting cables.

A simple cable to try is as follows:
Cast on a multiple of 4 sts + 2
Row 1 knit
Row 2 purl
Row 3 k1 (sl2 sts to cn, hold in front, k2, k2 from cn) to last stitch k1
Row 4 purl
Repeat Rows 1–4
(a similar cable pattern is used in the central pillow on pages 48–49)

When you have a sample of knitting you like see page 138 for instructions on how to work out your gauge. Then you can plan how to knit something of a specific size.

Designing patterns

Patterns are created by altering and combining different stitches, yarns, or colors. You can of course do all of these at once, but to keep it chic make it as simple as possible. I try to stick to the rule that three elements of a design is enough. If there are more than this it can look confusing as each element loses some of its strength. A single design element is anything from a novelty yarn to a stripe to a pretty trim—anything that is a designed feature rather than just the absolute basic requirements for the design.

These pillows are all the same tones and size—the only difference is the stitch pattern, which counts as one element of design. As you can see, texture is so important as it makes such a different impact, but in a clever way, and the group still works beautifully as a set.

From left to right the pillows show extra long stitch (see page 47), zig-zag stitch (see pages 50–51 for full pattern), cables (for an example see page 47), X pattern (see pages 52–55 for full pattern), and lace holes (for an example see page 47).

zig-zag pillow cover

Also shown on page 48, this zig-zag patterned pillow cover uses a simple stitch combination that creates the illusion of a geometric weave rather than knitting. By playing with the structure to make designs this clean looking, knitted projects can hold their own in any contemporary interior.

What you need

- size US 10 (6mm) needles
- Debbie Bliss Rialto Chunky yarn (*we used 6 balls of color 002*)
- a 15" (38cm) square pillow form
- a big button

What you do

The front

This should measure about 14¼" (36cm) x 14¼" (36cm). See page 130 for instructions on KB and PB.

Cast on 68 sts

Rows 1 and 2 purl

Row 3 sl1 wyib k1 (KB k1) x22

Row 4 sl1 wyif, purl to end

Row 5 sl1 wyib k2 (KB k1) x21, k2

Row 6 sl1 wyif, purl to end

Row 7 sl1 wyib (KB k1) x22, k1

Row 8 sl1 wyif p1 (p1 PB) x21, p3

Row 9 sl 1 wyib, knit to end

Row 10 sl1 wyif PB (p1 PB) x21, p2

Row 11 as Row 9

Row 12 sl1 wyif (p1 PB) x22, p1

Row 13 as Row 9

Row 14 as Row 8

Row 15 as Row 7

Row 16 as Row 4

Rows 3 – 16 is one repeat. Do 3 more full repeats. Then repeat Rows 3 – 12. Bind off purlwise

The back underlap

This measures about 11¾" (30cm) wide x 14¼" (36cm) high

Cast on 46 sts

Row 1 purl

Row 2 sl1 wyif, purl to end

Row 3 sl1 wyib, knit to end

Row 4–71 repeat Rows 2 – 3

Bind off knitwise

The back overlap with buttonhole

This measures about 7¼" (18.5cm) wide x 14¼" (36cm) high

Cast on 28 sts

Row 1 purl

Row 2 sl1 wyif, purl to end

Row 3 sl1 wyib, knit to end

Rows 4–71 repeat Rows 2 – 3 *

*on Row 35 knit 3 stitches then make a 6st buttonhole (see page 138). Bind off knitwise

To sew up see page 139. Sew button to underlap, aligning with buttonhole.

x pattern pillow cover

This is the sister pattern for the zig-zag pillow cover (see previous pages) but has more advanced technique in the middle, so master the zig-zag first. The technique for this is venturing into the realm of what I think of as "purist" knitting, the re-thinking of how we expect things to work in order to make something beautiful, new, and perfect—even if it does look deceptively simple when finished. Go on, challenge yourself!

What you need

- size US 10 (6mm) needles
- Debbie Bliss Rialto Chunky (*we used 6 balls of color 002*)
- a 15" (38cm) square pillow form
- a big button

What you do

The front

This should measure 14" (35.5cm) wide x 13" (33cm) long — always make pillow covers a bit- small or they look baggy. See page 130 for instructions on KB and PB.

Cast on 67 sts

Row 1 purl

Row 2 purl

Row 3 sl1 wyib k1 (k1 KB) x10, k35

Row 4 sl1 wyif p1 (p1 PB) x10, p35

Row 5 sl1 wyib (KB k1) x11, k33

Row 6 sl1 wyif (PB p1) x11, p33

Row 7 sl1 wyib (k1 KB) x11, k33

Row 8 sl1 wyif (p1 PB) x11, p33

Rows 9 – 38 repeat Rows 3 – 8

Row 39 slip all the stitches onto the other needle and cut the yarn leaving a long end for sewing. Take your yarn again and start from this end. Because you have slipped the stitches instead of knitting them they may be hanging on the needle the wrong way around — you may have to turn each stitch before you work it as otherwise it may end up with a twist in it which won't look so good.

Row 40 sl1 wyif p33 (PB p1) x11

Row 41 sl1 wyib k33 (KB k1) x11

Row 42 sl1 wyif p33 (p1 PB) x10, p3

Row 43 sl1 wyib k33 (k1 KB) x10, k3

Row 44 sl1 wyif p32 (PB p1) x11, p1

Row 45 sl1 wyib k32 (KB k1) x11, k1

Rows 46 – 75 repeat Rows 40 – 45

Bind off purlwise

For the back instructions see the Zig-Zag pillow cover pattern on page 50.

To sew up see page 139. Sew button to underlap, aligning with buttonhole.

The X pillow cover is shown here with the patchwork blanket (see pages 74–77) and patchwork pillow cover (see pages 30–32), showing how different styles can contrast in an interesting way. If you like the clean lines of the zig-zag and X pillows and want a patchwork blanket to match you could create one that incorporates the pillow fronts as panels within the patchwork.

apple-pie pillow cover

I call this the apple-pie cable as it reminds me of the latticed pastry on top of an apple pie. It's also a cozy, homely and warm cable, perfect for curling up on the sofa on winter nights.

What you need
- size US 10½ (6.5mm) needles
- Debbie Bliss Rialto Chunky Yarn (*we used 12 balls of color 003*)
- a 20" (5cm) square pillow form
- 3 lovely big buttons
- a cable needle (cn)

What you do
The front
This should measure about 19" (48cm) x 19" (48cm) — always make pillow covers small or they can look baggy. The stitch guage in cable pattern is 61/4 sts/in and 6¾ rows/in.

Cast on 118 sts
Row 1 purl
Row 2 purl
Row 3 sl1 wyib k2 sl2 wyib k108 sl2 wyib k3
Row 4 sl1 wyif p2 sl2 wyif p108 sl2 wyif p3
Row 5 sl1 wyib (sl2 to cn, hold in back, k1, k2 from cn, sl1 to cn, hold in front, k2 k1 from cn; this is called Bird Cable) k4 (sl4 to cn, hold in front k4, k4 from cn; this is called 8st Cable Front) x6, (sl4 to cn and hold in back, k4, k4 from cn; this is called 8st Cable Back) x6, k4 (Bird Cable) k1
Row 6 sl1 wyif purl to end
Row 7 as Row 3
Row 8 as Row 4
Row 9 sl1 wyib (Bird Cable) k104 (Bird Cable) k1
Row 10 as Row 6
Row 11 sl1 wyib k2 sl2 wyib k2 (8st Cable Back) x6, k8 (8st Cable Front) x6, k2 sl2 wyib k3
Row 12 as Row 4
Row 13 as Row 9
Row 14 as Row 6
Row 15 – 122 repeat Rows 3 – 14
Row 123 – 127 repeat Rows 3 – 7
Bind off knitwise

For the back instructions see the patchwork pillow cover pattern on page 32.

To sew up see page 139. Sew buttons to underlap, aligning with buttonholes.

On the side of the pillow you can see the structure of the apple-pie cable alongside the bird cable edging. This adds subtlety and finish to what is an otherwise simple design.

Finding good buttons . . .

. . . is much harder than you might expect, so pick them up when you find them. We especially love big vintage buttons and toggles, which will make the back of pillows just as pretty as the front.

geometric cable throw

This is about 74³/₄" (190cm) long and not for the faint hearted but is very rewarding when it's finished! We fringed ours randomly — follow the fringing instructions on page 110 if you'd like to do this too, allow for extra wool.

What you need

- 7mm (size 2) circular needles
- Rowan British Sheep Breeds Chunky Undyed (*we used 20 balls of color 954*)
- a cable needle (cn)

VARIATIONS

If you like the pattern of this but don't like the chunkiness or yarn then why not decide your own yarn, needles and size. The repeat widthways is 64 stitches and then you need to add 4 stitches for the edges. Knit yourself a sample with your preferred needles and yarn and use the repeat instructions to work out how many stitches and rows you need. You could do a really fine version or a smaller version and make a pillow cover — whatever you feel like is possible. Just be cautious that open loose knitting doesn't generally look good cabled, so keep stitches tight.

What you do

Cast on 196 sts — you definitely need circular needles for all these stitches!

Row 1 purl

Row 2 purl

Row 3 (and all other non-cable odd rows) knit

Row 4 (and every even row) purl

Row 5 K2 [(sl4 to cn and hold in back, k4, k4 from cn; this is called Cable Back) x4, (sl4 to cn and hold in front, k4, k4 from cn; this is called Cable Front) x4] x3, k2

Row 11 k2 [k4 (Cable Front) k4 (Cable Back) x2, (Cable Front) x2, k4 (Cable Back) k4] x3, k2

Row 17 as Row 5

Row 23 k2 [(Cable Back) k4 (Cable Front) k4 (Cable Back) (Cable Front) k4 (Cable Back) k4 (Cable Front)] x3, k2

Row 29 as Row 5

Row 35 k2 [(Cable Back) x2, k4 (Cable Front) k8 (Cable Back) k4 (Cable Front) x2] x3, k2

Row 41 as Row 5

Row 45 k2 [(Cable Front) x 4 (Cable Back) x 4] x3, k2

Row 51 k2 [(Cable Front) x2, k4 (Cable Back) k8 (Cable Front) k4 (Cable Back) x2] x3, k2

Row 57 as Row 45

Row 63 k2 [(Cable Front) k4 (Cable Back) k4 (Cable Front) (Cable Back) k4 (Cable Front) k4 (Cable Back)] x3, k2

Row 69 as Row 45

Row 75 k2 [k4 (Cable Back) k4 (Cable Front) x2, (Cable Back) x2, k4 (Cable Front) k4] x3, k2

Row 81 as Row 45

Rows 82 – 321 repeat Rows 2 – 81

Bind off knitwise

This huge cable repeat doesn't become clear until you see it on such a big scale and the full pattern reveals itself. We added a random fringe to soften this otherwise uniform design, but you could also add a fabric back or even knit a plain one to make a double-sided throw.

Sometimes you'll want your pattern to cover only part of your knitting, or to have sections of different patterns across a piece to create more complicated designs. To plan this you need to be methodical and the results should be perfect—whether it's a patterned stripe on a plain background or a "patchwork" blanket of different patterns that is actually knitted in one piece.

COMBINING PATTERNS

Decide what patterns you would like to use, knit a sample and work out your guage for each (following the instructions on page 138). If you're using cables just measure the width of your sample cable. It will make life a lot easier if you pick patterns that are all knitted on the same size needles with the same yarn.

You can play around with your samples to see how the patterns look together and do some sketches of what kind of layout you would like the final piece to have. Start with a simple shape, like a pillow or a throw, and decide the size. Then start to plan how much you'd like to cover with each pattern across the width. Think also about whether you would like some kind of detail on the edge, and include this in your planning if you do. You can then follow the instructions on pages 141–143 to design your final full pattern.

bolster pillow

This bolster pillow is a perfect example of combining textures in one piece effectively. Using different textures but keeping the shape and yarn simple like this will create something truly striking for any style of interior.

We worked out this the pattern for a bolster pillow using the method described on pages 141–142

What you need

- size US 9 (5.5mm) needles
- a cable needle (cn)
- Patons Merino Wool DK (*we used 7 balls of color 92*)
- a pillow form about 24" (60cm) wide x 11" (30cm) high
- 2 big buttons

Pattern layout

8st Cables — short arrow direction indicates cable direction
NB Average row gauge = 6½r/in — you need this to work out length

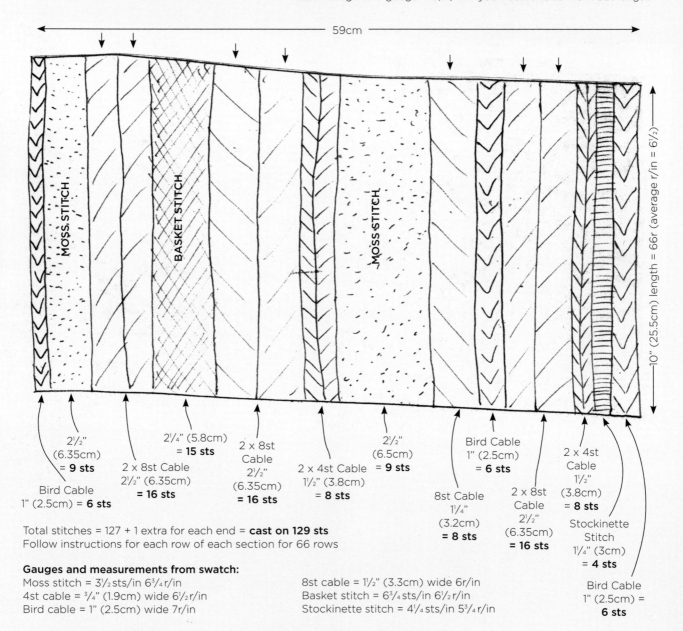

59cm

10" (25.5cm) length = 66r (average r/in = 6½)

MOSS STITCH

BASKET STITCH

MOSS STITCH

2½" (6.35cm) = **9 sts**

Bird Cable 1" (2.5cm) = **6 sts**

2 x 8st Cable 2½" (6.35cm) = **16 sts**

2¼" (5.8cm) = **15 sts**

2 x 8st Cable 2½" (6.35cm) = **16 sts**

2 x 4st Cable 1½" (3.8cm) = **8 sts**

2½" (6.5cm) = **9 sts**

8st Cable 1¼" (3.2cm) = **8 sts**

Bird Cable 1" (2.5cm) = **6 sts**

2 x 8st Cable 2½" (6.35cm) = **16 sts**

2 x 4st Cable 1½" (3.8cm) = **8 sts**

Stockinette Stitch 1¼" (3cm) = **4 sts**

Bird Cable 1" (2.5cm) = **6 sts**

Total stitches = 127 + 1 extra for each end = **cast on 129 sts**
Follow instructions for each row of each section for 66 rows

Gauges and measurements from swatch:

Moss stitch = 3½ sts/in 6¾ r/in
4st cable = ¾" (1.9cm) wide 6½ r/in
Bird cable = 1" (2.5cm) wide 7r/in

8st cable = 1½" (3.3cm) wide 6r/in
Basket stitch = 6¾ sts/in 6½ r/in
Stockinette stitch = 4¼ sts/in 5¾ r/in

Contrasting color makes the bolster pillow (below) at home on this lemon-colored chair, whilst the Super Easy Bedthrow seen on the previous pages (see page 16 for the pattern) complements the more organic aspects of the interior.

What you do

This cover is knitted using two ends (balls) of yarn at once. See page 130 for instructions on KB and PB.

Front Panel (about 23¼" [59cm] x 10" [25.5cm])

Cast on (using two balls at once) 129 sts

Row 1 purl

Row 2 purl

Row 3 sl1 wyib k2 sl2 wyib k32 sl2 wyib k10 (k1 p1) x4, k25 (KB) x7, k17 (k1 p1) x4, k3 sl2 wyib k3

Row 4 sl1 wyif p2 sl2 wyif p27 (PB) x7, p44 sl2 wyif p32 sl2 wyif p3

Row 5 sl1 wyib (sl2 to cn, hold in back, k1, k2 from cn, sl1 to cn, hold in front, k2, k1 from cn; this is called Bird Cable) k4 (sl2 to cn, hold in back, k2, k2 from cn; this is called 4st Cable Back) (sl2 to cn, hold in front, k2, k2 from cn; this is called 4st Cable Front) k16 (Bird Cable) k8 (p1 k1) x4, p1 (4st Cable Back) (4st Cable Front) k16 (KB) x7, k17 (p1 k1) x4, p1 (Bird Cable) k1

Row 6 sl1 wyif p31, (PB) x7, purl to end

Row 7 sl1 wyib k2 sl2 wyib k14 (sl4 to cn, hold in back, k4, k4 from cn; this is called 8st Cable Back) x2, k2 sl2 wyib k2 (sl4 to cn, hold in front, k4, k4 from cn; this is called 8st Cable Front) (k1 p1) x4, k9 (8st Cable Back) (8st Cable Front) (KB)

x7, k1 (8st Cable Back) x2, (k1 p1)
x4, k3 sl2 wyib k3

Row 8 as Row 4

Row 9 as Row 5

Row 10 as Row 6

Rows 11 – 66 repeat Rows 3–10

Bind off knitwise

Back Underlap
**(10½" [26.5cm] wide x 10½"
[26.5cm] long)**

Cast on 44 sts (using 2 balls at once)

Row 1 purl

Row 2 sl1 wyif purl to end

Row 3 sl1 wyib knit to end

Rows 4–59 repeat Rows 2–3

Bind off knitwise

Back Overlap
**(15½" [40cm] wide x 10½" [26
cm] long)**

Cast on 66 sts (using two balls at
once)

Row 1 purl

Row 2 sl1 wyif purl to end

Row 3 sl1 wyib knit to end

Rows 4–59 repeat Rows 2–3*

Bind off knitwise

* On Rows 15 and 45 make a 5st
buttonhole 4 sts into the row
(see page 138 for how to make
buttonholes). To sew up see page
139. Sew buttons to underlap,
aligning with buttonholes.

patchwork blanket

This blanket was made using yarns found throughout this book, but of course you can substitute these for whatever suits your home—multicolored and multitextural, or shades of one color in the same yarn for a more minimal look. The possibilities are endless.

What you do

Border pieces

There are 4 of these pieces—2 long and 2 short. The longer ones measure 60" (152.5cm) wide to start and grows to 66¾" (169.5cm) at Row 19. The shorter ones are 40" (101.5cm) wide to start and grows to 46¼" (119cm) at row 19. Both are 6¼" (16cm) long overall. Using chocolate (shade 10) Patons Wool Blend Aran and size US 7 (4.5mm) needles cast on 285/190 sts. Stitch gauge 4¾ sts/in and 6r/in

Rows 1 and 2 purl

Row 3 sl1 wyib k2 yo knit to last 3 sts yo k3 (287/192 sts)

When working the yo make sure they have twists and do not create lace holes (see page 136).

Row 4 sl1 wyif p2 yo purl to last 3 sts yo p3 (289/194 sts)

Rows 5 – 18 as Rows 3 – 4 (317/222 sts)

Row 19 knit

Row 20 purl

Row 21 sl1 wyib k2 k2tog knit to last 5 sts, k2tog k3 (315/220 sts)

Row 22 sl1 wyif p2 p2tog purl to last 5 sts p2tog p3 (313/218 sts)

Row 23 – 36 as Rows 21 – 22 (285/190 sts)

Row 37 knit

Bind off knitwise

Piece 1

24" (61cm) wide x 35½" (90.5cm) long. See page 130 for instructions on KB and PB. Using blue Debbie Bliss Rialto Chunky and size US 10½ (6.5mm) needles cast on 90 sts. Stitch gauge 3¾ sts/in and 4¾r/in

Rows 1 and 2 purl

Row 3 knit

Row 4 – 9 as Rows 2 – 3

Row 10 p1 PB x44, p1

Row 11 k2 KB x43, k2

Row 12 – 61 repeat Rows 2 – 11

Rows 62 – 169 repeat Rows 2 – 9

Bind off knitwise

Piece 2

12" (31cm) wide x 15¾" (40cm) long. Using beige Debbie Bliss Amalfi and size US 6 (4mm) needles cast on 66 sts. Stitch gauge 5½ sts/in and 7¾r/in

Rows 1 and 2 purl

Row 3 knit

Row 4 – 11 as Rows 2 – 3

Row 12 knit

Row 13 purl

Row 14 – 17 as Rows 12 – 13

Row 18 – 121 repeat rows 2 – 17

Bind off knitwise

Piece 3

8" (20.5cm) wide x 31½" (80cm) long. Using black Rowan Big Wool and size US 15 (10mm) needles cast on 24 sts. Stitch gauge 3 sts/in (You'll also need a cable needle)

Rows 1 and 2 purl

Row 3 knit

Row 4 purl

Row 5 k2 (sl3 to cn, hold in back k3, k3 from cn, k1) x2, sl3 to cn, hold in front, k3, k3 from cn, k2

Row 6 purl

Row 7 knit

Repeat Rows 2 – 7 until you have a piece 32" (81.5 cm) long and then bind off knitwise

Piece 4

8" (20.5cm) wide x 20" (51cm) long. Using marled brown (shade 14)

continued on page 76

Patons Wool Blend Aran and size US 7 (4.5mm) needles cast on 38 sts. Stitch gauge 4¾ sts/in.

Rows 1 and 2 purl

Row 3 knit

Repeat Rows 2–3 until you have a piece 20" (51cm) long and then bind off knitwise

Piece 5

8" (20.5cm) wide x 8" (20.5cm) long. Using gray (shade 92) Patons Merino DK and size US 6 (4mm) needles cast on 40 sts. Stitch gauge 5 sts/in.

Rows 1 and 2 purl

Row 3 knit

Repeat Rows 2–3 until you have a piece 8" (20.5cm) long and then bind off knitwise

Piece 6

4" (10cm) wide by 12¼" (31cm) long. Using lilac Debbie Bliss Rialto Chunky and size US 10½ (6.5mm) needles cast on 15 sts. Stitch gauge 3¾ sts/in and 5¼r/in

Rows 1-64 purl

Bind off purlwise

Piece 7

16¾" (42.5cm) wide x 38½" (98cm) long. Using Rowan British Sheep Breeds undyed DK and size US 6 (4mm) needles cast on 88 sts. Stitch gauge 5¼ sts/in.

Row 1 (k2 p2) x22

Row 2 p1 (k2 p2) x21, k2 p1

Repeat rows 1–2 until you have a piece 38½" (98cm) long then bind off knitwise

Piece 8

16¼" (41cm) wide x 12" (30.5cm) long. Using gray (shade 92) Patons Merino DK and size US 9 (5.5mm) needles cast on 89 sts using 2 balls at once. Stitch gauge 5½ sts/in and 5½r/in. (You'll need a cable needle.)

Rows 1 and 2 purl

Row 3 k9 (k1 p1) x4, k25 (KB) x7, k17 (k1 p1) x4, k3 sl2 wyib k3

Row 4 sl1 wyif p2 sl2 wyif p27 PB x7, purl to end

Row 5 k9 (p1 k1) x4, p1 (sl2 to cn, hold in back, k2, k2 from cn; this is called 4st cable back) (sl2 to cn, hold in front, k2, k2 from cn; this is called 4st cable front) k16 (KB) x7, k17 (p1 k1) x4, p1 (sl2 to cn, hold in back, k1, k2 from cn, sl1 to cn, hold in front, k2, k1 from cn; this is called bird cable) k1

Row 6 sl1 wyif p31 (PB) x7, purl to end

Row 7 k1 (sl4 to cn, hold in front, k4, k4 from cn; this is called 8st cable front) (k1 p1) x4, k9 (sl4 to cn, hold in back, k4, k4 from cn; this is called 8st cable back) (8st cable front) (KB) x7, k1 (8st cable back) x2, (k1 p1) x4, k3 sl2 wyib k3

Row 8 as Row 4

Row 9 as Row 5

Row 10 as Row 6

Row 11–66 repeat Rows 3–10

Bind off knitwise

Piece 9

8" (20.5cm) wide x 8" (20.5cm) long. Using gray (shade 92) Patons Merino DK and size US 6 (4mm) needles cast on 44 sts. Stitch gauge 5½ sts/in and 7½r/in.

Rows 1–60 knit

Bind off knitwise

Piece 10

4" (10cm) wide x 4" (10cm) long. Using black Rowan Big Wool and 7mm (size 2) needles cast on 13 sts. (No exact US equivalent: between US sizes 10.5 and 11 needles). Adjust needle size if necessary to obtain the correct gauge. Stitch gauge 3¼ sts/in and 4¼r/in.

Row 1 knit

Row 2 purl

Row 3–16 repeat Rows 1–2

Bind off knitwise

Piece 11

8" (20.5cm) wide x 8¼" (21cm) long. Using burgundy Debbie Bliss Rialto Chunky and size US 10½ (6.5mm) needles cast on 30 sts. Stitch gauge 3¾ sts/in and 4¾r/in.

Rows 1–8 (k5 p5) x3

Row 9–11 (p5 k5) x3

Row 12–19 as Rows 1–8

Row 20–26 as Rows 9–11

Row 27–30 as Rows 1–8

Row 31–35 as Rows 9–11

Row 36–38 as Rows 1–8

Bind off purlwise

Lay the pieces out as shown opposite. Sew everything together except the border. Pin the ends of the borders together and sew up so you have a rectangle. Lay right sides together on the blanket and whipstitch through the front layer only. Fold the border over to the back of the piece and sew in place.

long border

short border

7

11

9

5

1

6

10

4

2

8

3

Inserting a contrasting yarn as a vertical panel

You can also add vertical stripes into knitting by changing your yarn. The proper name for this is "intarsia" and it is often used to create pictures on sweaters (this is the technique used to create novelty or themed sweaters, such as reindeers at Christmas). The technique is actually quite under developed, but enormously satisfying and beautiful when you've cracked it.

The basic theory is that as you work along the row instead of allocating different stitch instructions to make the sections you change yarns. Each section will need its own ball and you'll need a system to keep them in order and untangled or total chaos will take over pretty quickly! I line them up on the floor around me and make sure I alternate the way I turn the knitting at the end of each row—it seems to work. For technical instructions see page 140.

intarsia blanket

About as far from a Christmas sweater as you can get, this beautiful intarsia blanket combines yarns of subtly different shades and weights resulting in a striking contemporary effect.

What you need

- size US 15 (10mm) needles
- Rowan Big Wool (*we used 5 balls of color 001*)
- Rowan British Sheep Breeds DK Undyed (*we used 9 balls of ecru*)

This blanket measures about 45½" (115.5cm) wide x 58¾" (149cm) long. Stitch gauge 2.75 sts/in 3.25 r/in.

What you do

Cast on 114 sts including yarn changes as follows — see page 140 for detailed instructions on how to achieve this

Big Wool (BW) cast on 18 sts
two balls of DK together (2 x DK) cast on 6 sts
BW cast on 30 sts
2 x DK cast on 6 sts
BW cast on 30 sts
2 x DK cast on 6 sts
BW cast on 18 sts

Row 1 Purl entire row changing from one yarn to the next as shown in the row beneath it

Row 2 Knit entire row changing from one yarn to the next as shown in the row beneath it

Rows 3–11 repeat Rows 1 and 2

Row 12 BW k6. Take the next 2 x DK (12st early) change over to the DK and k30. Take the BW (12st late) change over to the BW and k6. Continue changing like this:
2 x DK k30
BW k6
2 x DK k30
BW k6
You will be left with 12-st wide floats (strands of yarn not included in the structure) but don't worry about these as they can be sewn in later. Try to leave a long end — it makes sewing in easier.

Rows 13–18 Continue following the yarn layout as established, knitting the even numbered rows and purling the odd numbered rows

Row 19 Changeover your yarns as you did before:
BW p18
2 x DK p6
BW p30
2 x DK p6
BW p30
2 x DK p6
BW p18

Rows 20–181 repeat Rows 2–19
Rows 182–191 repeat Rows 2–11
Bind off purlwise.

We fringed the ends of ours carrying on the yarns in the pattern — see page 110 for instructions for adding fringe.

lacy panel

This panel uses a series of different repeats that create an impressive overall effect. As long as you complete each repeat before moving onto the next the pattern will work out. To make your piece longer you can do more of whichever repeat you like. To make it wider cast on more repeats widthways. You can create as many repeats as necessary to suit your chosen space, but what we did is written in *italics*.

What you need

- size US 6 (4mm) needles
- Patons Linen Shadow DK (*we used 8 balls of color 102*)

What you do

Cast on a multiple of 24 sts + 7. (*We cast on 79 sts*) You may wish to do a single repeat for a few rows first to check how wide it is — ours was 4¼" (11cm) wide + 1½" (4cm) for the 7 edge stitches (14¼" [36cm] wide overall).

Row 1 purl

Row 2 purl

Section 1 (2 row repeat)

Row 1 sl1 wyib KB k1 (yo k10 sl1 wyib k2tog psso k10 yo k1) x3, k3

Row 2 sl1 wyif PB purl to end (and all even rows in the whole pattern) Repeat Rows 1–2 for desired length. Using these needles and yarn you can expect 6 r/in (*we did 72 rows*).

We did this section making sure the yo stitches were worked with twists to close the lace holes (see page 136). If you prefer you can work without twists to create lace holes.

Section 2 (44 row repeat)

Row 1 sl1 wyib KB k1 (yo k10 sl1 wyib k2tog psso k10 yo k1) x3, k3

Row 3 sl1 wyib KB k1 (k1 yo k9 sl1 wyib k2tog psso k9 yo k2) x3, k3

Row 5 sl1 wyib KB k1 (k2 yo k8 sl1 wyib K2tog psso k8 yo k3) x3, k3

Row 7 sl1 wyib KB k1 (k3 yo k7 sl1 wyib k2tog psso k7 yo k4) x3, k3

Row 9 sl1 wyib KB k1 (k4 yo k6 sl1 wyib k2tog psso k6 yo k5) x3, k3

Row 11 sl1 wyib KB k1 (k5 yo k5 sl1 wyib k2tog psso k5 yo k6) x3, k3

Row 13 sl1 wyib KB k1 (k6 yo k4 sl1 wyib k2tog psso k4 yo k7) x3, k3

Row 15 sl1 wyib KB k1 (k7 yo k3 sl1 wyib k2tog psso k3 yo k8) x3, k3

Row 17 sl1 wyib KB k1 (k8 yo k2 sl1 wyib k2tog psso k2 yo k9) x3, k3

Row 19 sl1 wyib KB k1 (k9 yo k1 sl1 wyib k2tog psso k1 yo k10) x3, k3

Row 21 sl1 wyib KB k1 (k10 yo sl1 wyib k2tog psso yo k11) x3, k3

Row 23 sl1 wyib KB k2tog k10 (yo k1 yo k10 sl1 wyib k2tog psso k10) x2, yo k1 yo k10 k2tog k3

Row 25 sl1 wyib KB k2tog k9 (yo k3 yo k9 sl1 wyib k2tog psso k9) x2, yo k3 yo k9 k2tog k3

Row 27 sl1 wyib KB k2tog k8 (yo k5 yo k8 sl1 wyib k2tog psso k8) x2, yo k5 yo k8 k2tog k3

Row 29 sl1 wyib KB k2tog k7 (yo k7 yo k7 sl1 wyib k2tog psso k7) x2, yo k7 yo k7 k2tog k3

Row 31 sl1 wyib KB k2tog k6 (yo k9 yo k6 sl1 wyib k2tog psso k6) x2, yo k9 yo k6 k2tog k3

Row 33 sl1 wyib KB k2tog k5 (yo k11 yo k5 sl1 wyib k2tog psso k5) x2, yo k11 yo k5 k2tog k3

Row 35 sl1 wyib KB k2tog k4 (yo k13 yo k4 sl1 wyib k2tog psso k4) x2, yo k13 yo k4 k2tog k3

Row 37 sl1 wyib KB k2tog k3 (yo k15 yo k3 sl1 wyib k2tog psso k3) x2, yo k15 yo k3 k2tog k3

Row 39 sl1 wyib KB k2tog k2 (yo k17 yo k2 sl1 wyib k2tog psso k2) x2, yo k17 yo k2 k2tog k3

continued on page 87

This lacy panel uses twisted and non-twisted yarn over stitches to great effect, creating a pattern that develops down the length of the piece and looks amazing. By referencing old-style lace café curtains this introduces a sense of the traditional, but presents it from a thoroughly modern aspect.

Row 41 sl1 wyib KB k2tog k1 (yo k19 yo k1 sl1 wyib k2tog psso k1) x2, yo k19 yo k1 k2tog k3

Row 43 sl1 wyib KB k2tog (yo k21 yo sl1 wyib k2tog psso) x2, yo k21 yo k2tog k3

We did two repeats of this (including the one above) with the yo worked with twists to close the lace holes. We then did two repeats working them without twists.

Section 3 (20 row repeat)

Row 1 sl1 wyib KB k1 (yo k4 sl1 wyib k2tog psso k4 yo k1) x6, k3

Row 3 sl1 wyib KB k1 (k1 yo k3 sl1 wyib k2tog psso k3 yo k2) x6, k3

Row 5 sl1 wyib KB k1 (k2 yo k2 sl1 wyib k2tog psso k2 yo k3) x6, k3

Row 7 sl1 wyib KB k1 (k3 yo k1 sl1 wyib k2tog psso k1 yo k4) x6, k3

Row 9 sl1 wyib KB k1 (k4 yo sl1 wyib k2tog psso yo k5) x6, k3

Row 11 sl1 wyib KB k2tog (k4 yo k1 yo k4 sl1 wyib k2tog psso) x5, k4 yo k1 yo k4 k2tog k3

Row 13 sl1 wyib KB k2tog (k3 yo k3 yo k3 sl1 wyib k2tog psso) x5, k3 yo k3 yo k3 k2tog k3

Row 15 sl1 wyib KB k2tog (k2 yo k5 yo k2 sl1 wyib k2tog psso) x5, k2 yo k5 yo k2 k2tog k3

Row 17 sl1 wyib KB k2tog (k1 yo k7 yo k1 sl1 wyib k2tog psso) x5, k1 yo k7 yo k1 k2tog k3

Row 19 sl1 wyib KB k2tog (yo k9 yo sl1 wyib k2tog psso) x5, k9 yo k2tog k3

We did 2 of these repeats working the yo with no twists.

Section 4 (2 row repeat)

Row 1 sl1 wyib KB (k1 yo k4 sl1 wyib k2tog psso k4 yo) x6, k4

We repeated these two rows for 28 rows without twists in the yo.

Section 5 (8 row repeat)

Row 1 sl1 wyib KB (k1 yo k1 sl1 wyib k2tog psso k1 yo) x12, k1 k3

Row 3 sl1 wyib KB (k2 yo sl1 wyib k2tog psso yo k1) x12, k4

Row 5 sl1 wyib KB k2tog (k1 yo k1 yo k1 sl1 wyib k2tog psso) x11, k1 yo k1 yo k1 k2tog k3

Row 7 sl1 wyib KB k2tog (yo k3 yo sl1 wyib k2tog psso) x11, yo k3 yo k2tog k3

We repeated this section 3 times (including the repeat above) without twists and 3 repeats with twists.

Section 6 (2 row repeat)

Row 1 sl1 wyib KB (k1 yo k1 sl1 wyib k2tog psso k1 yo) x12, k4

We repeated these 2 rows for 48 rows with twists.

To finish

Row 1 knit
Row 2 purl
Row 3 knit
Row 4 purl
Row 5 knit
Bind off knitwise.

When you've finished you need to give your panel a good steam (see page 140). Then find a thin piece of wooden dowel the same length as the width of your piece and lay it against the top plain section of the panel. Wrap the top over the dowel and sew it down. You can then put a hanging loop in and hang your panel.

Our panel is 14³⁄₄" (36cm) wide and 68³⁄₄" (165cm) long.

There is something very comforting about interior spaces that have knitted details. They add a certain warmth and charm so welcome in a home. However it is likely that most things you have already will not be knitted, so it's important to consider how your knitted pieces will fit into your existing space so that it works as a whole.

BESPOKE KNITTING FOR YOUR HOME

Luckily it's really easy to plan how to cover something with a little measuring and some simple math—it's only a small step beyond everything covered so far in this book. The key now though is accurate planning and thought for the design of your piece—if you're covering a chair, for example, it will take a long time, use a lot of yarn and you will have to live with it when it's finished. I strongly recommend taking time to consider how the color, texture and pattern will work within the room. Using your samples, try out your ideas in the space before getting started. Remember, if you're doing something large a strong design will be far more dominant on that scale instead of the small swatch you have in your hand so imagination and vision are vital at this point. Sometimes photographs of your space can help reduce the scale and show more easily how your new design will fit in scale wise. You can use whatever technique you find helpful to visualize the finished result—just go for it.

doorstop

Although extremely easy this is the perfect introduction to creating a knit that fits a solid object. It also introduces the idea of knitting with tougher materials – a perfect alternative for items where conventional yarns aren't as suitable.

What you need

- something square and heavy to cover (we used a piece of wood)
- size US 10½ to 15 (6.5 to 10 mm) (the exact size is up to you)
- some chunky yarn (*we used Rowan Big Wool in color 001*)
- some raffia, linen tape, or something similar

OBJECTS MADE OF SQUARES OR RECTANGLES

If the object you wish to cover is made up of flat sides with right angles then you can use everything you've learned to design each panel, which when sewn together will fit snugly. Now is when you need to think about what the edges of any open sides will look like and where you want to place your patterns on the object. Take it little by little and you'll be fine

---

What you do

Measure each side of your block and plan how many stitches and rows you need for each panel, using your stitch gauge worked out from a sample as described on page 138. You can then either knit each panel individually and sew each side up or add some together (for example, the four around the outside could be knitted in one strip) so you have fewer seams. If your knit is open and exposes the block you may need to paint the block or make a fabric cover of the same or a contrasting color to show through the knit.

Our version has a 6¾" (17cm) square cube and has the following panels:

Panel 1

Using Rowan Big Wool cast on 21 sts and alternate knit and purl for 24 rows.

Panels 2, 3 and 4

Using Rowan Big Wool cast on 21 sts and alternate knit and purl for 12 rows. Change to raffia and continue for another 12 rows.

Panel 5

Using raffia cast on 21 sts and alternate knit and purl for 24 rows.

We added a tough burlap panel on the base but you could do another of the panels with both yarns and it could be used whichever way up you choose. Simply sew the panels together and pull over the block before sewing it in.

cabled footstool

To complement more traditional furniture you might consider a busy pattern like this. However, if your taste is simpler then you can pare it down as you like. This footstool is essentially made of flat panels like the doorstop, albeit far more complicated ones.

What you need

- size US 6 (4mm) needles
- Rowans British Sheep Breeds yarn (we used about 4 balls of color 780 Ecru)
- a footstool

The footstool we used measured 15¾" (40cm) wide by 11¾" (30cm) long on the top and approximately 3¼" (8.5cm) high. You can always alter the size of the pieces (quantity of cables/repeats and so on) to make yours fit.

Each panel uses a variety of stitches and was designed in the same way as the bolster cushion (see pages 68–73), demonstrating how by combining techniques you can create an impressive design step by step. The full drawings and calculations are shown on page 141 for your reference.

What you do

The top

Ours measured 15¼" (38.7cm) wide x 11½" (29cm) long

Cast on 126 sts

Row 1 purl

Row 2 purl

Row 3 sl1 wyib (KB) x12, k76 (KB) x12, k1

Row 4 (and all other even rows) sl1 wyif p1 (PB) x11, p78 (PB) x11, p2

Row 5 sl1 wyib (KB) x12, k1 (sl2 to cn, hold in back, k2, k2 from cn; this is called 4st Cable Back) k66 (sl2 to cn, hold in front, k2, k2 from cn; this is called 4st Cable Front) k1 (KB) x12, k1

Row 7 sl 1 wyib (KB) x12, k6 (sl4 to cn, hold in back, k4, k4 from cn; this is called 8st Cable Back) x8, k6 (KB) x12, k1

Row 9 as Row 5

Row 11 as Row 3

Row 13 sl1 wyib (KB) x12, k1 4st Cable Back k5 (sl4 to cn, hold in front, k4, k4 from cn; this is called 8st Cable Front) x7, k5 4st Cable Front k1 (KB) x12, k1

Rows 15–86 repeat Rows 3–14

Rows 87–94 repeat Rows 3–10

Bind off purlwise.

The side trim

Ours measured 2¾" (7cm) wide and 53" (134.5cm) long

Cast on 24 sts

Row 1 purl

Row 2 purl

Row 3 sl1 wyib KB k13 (sl2 wyib k2) x2

Row 4 sl1 wyif p1 sl2 wyif p2 sl2 wyif purl to end

Row 5 sl1 wyib KB k12 (sl1 to cn, hold in back, k1, k1 from cn, sl1 to cn, hold in front, k1, k1 from cn; this is called Small Bird Cable) x2, k1

Row 6 sl1 wyif purl to end

Row 7 sl1 wyib KB (sl3 to cn, hold in back, k3, k3 from cn, sl3 to cn, hold in front, k3, k3 from cn; this is called Double Cable Pointing Down) k1 (sl2 wyib k2) x2

Row 8 as Row 4

Row 9 as Row 5

Row 10 as Row 6

Row 11 as Row 3

continued on page 97

Row 12 as Row 4

Row 13 sl1 wyib KB Double Cable Pointing Down (Small Bird Cable) x2, k1

Row 14 as Row 6

Row 15 – 62 repeat Rows 3 – 14 Continue to repeat Rows 3 – 6, working (sl3 to cn, hold in front, k3, k3 from cn, sl3 to cn, hold in back, k3, k3 from cn; this is called Double Cable Pointing Up) or Double Cable Pointing Down on the indicated rows

Double Cable pointing up
Rows 77, 83, 89, 95, 101, 107, 113, 119, 125, 131
End of section 1b Row 135 [15" (38cm)]

Double Cable pointing down
Rows 139, 145, 151, 157, 163, 169, 175, 181
End of section 2a Row 185 [20¾" (52.5cm)]

Double Cable pointing up
Rows 189, 195, 201, 207, 213, 219, 225, 231
End of section 2b Row 235 [26½" (67.5cm)]

Double Cable pointing down
Rows 239, 245, 251, 257, 263, 269, 275, 281, 287, 293
End of section 3a Row 301 [34" (86.5cm)]

Double Cable pointing up
Rows 309, 315, 321, 327, 333, 339, 345, 351, 357, 363
End of section 3b Row 367 [41½" (105.5cm)]

Double Cable pointing down
Rows 371, 377, 383, 389, 395, 401, 407, 413
End of section 4a Row 417 [47¼" (120cm)]

Double Cable pointing up
Rows 421, 427, 433, 439, 445, 451, 457, 463
End of piece Row 467 [53" (134.5cm)]
Bind off knitwise

Sew the ends of the side trim together first, then match up the corner details of this strip to the corners of the top and sew the two parts together. We pulled our cover on and sewed a line of running stitches around the hem to fix it to the stool securely, but if you just want to pull it on then make your side trim a bit wider and shorter than the stool and it will cling on.

cushions for chairs

To make this chair cover we designed it little by little. It is easier to select furniture that has removable cushions so you can measure them and fit the knitted covers more easily. For this chair we kept it simple and made two panels the same width, one long enough to stretch up and over the back and the other to cover the top, front and back edges of the seat pad. Measure each part you want to cover and work out the panel width accordingly. You can work out the length at this stage or just keep knitting until it's long enough.

What you need
- size US 10½ (6.5mm) needles
- cable needle
- Rowans Felted Tweed Chunky (*we used 12 balls 283 Pebble*)

What you do
The cable section is a fixed pattern and is 7½" (19cm) / 34 sts wide, but you can adapt the width of the bumpy edges—the stitch gauge for this is 3 sts/in (*we used 19 sts for each edge*)

Chair Back
Cast on necessary number of sts (*we cast on 72 sts*)

Rows 1 and 2 purl

Row 3 (purl number of stitches you are using for the bumpy edge then turn your piece, knit the same number of stitches, turn, purl same stitches, turn, knit same stitches, turn, look over your piece to the back and use your right needle to pick up the purl stitch directly below the first stitch on your left needle, lift this stitch up onto your left needle and knit this and the original first stitch together; repeat this for all your edge stitches; this is called Ridge) k34 (Ridge)

Row 4 purl

Row 5 knit ridge sts k1 (sl4 to cn, hold in back, k4, k4 from cn; this is called 8st Cable Back) x2, (sl4 to cn, hold in front, k4, k4 from cn; this is called 8st Cable Front) x2, k1 knit ridge sts

Row 6 purl

Row 7 (Ridge) k34 (Ridge)

Row 8 purl

Row 9 knit

Row 10 purl

Row 11 (Ridge) k5 (8st Cable Front) k8 (8st Cable Back) k5 (Ridge)

Row 12 purl

Row 13 knit

Row 14 purl

Row 15 (Ridge) k34 (Ridge)

Row 16 purl

Rows 5–16 is one repeat—do as many of these as you need.

For the seat pad we made a plain piece of knitting big enough to cover the base and the sides. The base was 24½" (62cm) wide by 19" (48.5cm) long. The seat pad was 2¾" (7cm) thick. It needed to be 30" (76cm) wide by 19" (48cm) for a snug fit. Reduce your total slightly when you've worked out what you need to achieve this. The gauge we used for our plain section was 3¼ sts/in (we cast on 95 sts).

Place the pieces on your pads. Pin them together with safety pins and either sew them together from the outside while on the cushion or slip them off, turn inside out, and sew up leaving one seam open. Pull the cover over and sew up the last seam from the outside. If you would like to easily remove your covers use this seam to add buttons or snaps.

The rich texture of the knit works so well in this minimal space. The pattern is strong and reflects the lines of the room.

circular place mat

This project is one that looks really impressive but is actually easy to knit. Once you've got the hang of knitting curves you could use it for a wide variety of items—not just our stylish reinvention of the humble doily!

What you need

- size US 6 (4mm) needles
- Rowan Pima Cotton DK (*we used 2 balls of color 057*)

SHAPING TO FIT CURVES

So far almost everything has been a variation of a square—flat with right angles and perfect for knit's grid-like structure. However, to fit different shapes you need to know how to shape your knitting. Basically this is done by decreasing or increasing a certain number of stitches on particular rows to grow and shrink your knitting according to the shape you want. To plan what to do, you need to measure your item and make a template of it on some paper. This doesn't have to be to scale, as long as the measurements are right. See the instructions on pages 142–143 to see how to convert these drawings into pattern instructions.

What you do

Cast on 24 sts

Row 1 purl

Row 2 (p1 yo p1 yo p1) x8 (40 sts)

Row 3 Double length knit (put your needle through to knit as normal but wind yarn around twice instead of once; work as a normal stitch on next row, which will release the long stitch)

Row 4 knit

Row 5 knit

Row 6 p1 (p2tog yo) to last st, p1

Row 7 purl

Row 8 (p1 yo p1 yo p1 yo p1 yo p1) x8 (72 sts)

Rows 9–15 repeat Rows 1–7 with the following exception: the equivalent to Row 2 is just purl with no yo from now on.

Row 16 (p1 yo p2 yo p1 yo p1 yo p1 yo p2 yo p1) x8 (120 sts)

Rows 17–23: repeat Rows 9–15

Row 24 (p2 yo p2 yo p2 yo p3 yo p2 yo p2 yo p2) x8 (168 sts)

Rows 25–31: repeat Rows 9–15

Row 32 (p3 yo p3 yo p3 yo p3 yo p3 yo p3 yo p3) x8 (216 sts)

Rows 33–39: repeat Rows 9–15

Row 40 (p4 yo p4 yo p4 yo p3 yo p4 yo p4 yo p4) x8 (264 sts)

Rows 41–47: repeat Rows 9–15

Row 48 (p4 yo p5 yo p5 yo p5 yo p5 yo p5 yo p4)x8 (312 sts)

Rows 49–55: repeat Rows 9–15

Row 56 (p6 yo p6 yo p5 yo p5 yo p5 yo p6 yo p6) x8 (360 sts)

Row 57 purl

Bind off knitwise

Your cast on measurement should be 4¼" (11cm). The length of each repeat should be 1¼" (3cm). Each repeat should add an extra 8½" (21.5cm) to the width of the piece. When you've knitted it simply fold it in half widthways, right sides together and sew down the seam. If you would like a bigger circle just continue knitting, increasing as shown with each repeat. Once your circle is sewn together then steam on the reverse (see page 140) to relax the stitches.

When you've made this once you'll realize that with this pattern you can easily adapt it to make small circles for coasters, larger ones for tablecloths, or at the other end of the scale alter your yarn to something substantial and increase your needle size to make a rug—you will need really long circular needles to hold all the stitches comfortably.

round pouffe

For this project we found a Moroccan-style pouffe approximately 21$\frac{1}{4}$" (54cm) across by 11$\frac{3}{4}$" (30cm) high. For a snug fit we made the cover smaller—20$\frac{1}{2}$" (52cm) by 9$\frac{1}{2}$" (24cm). As the knit is pulled taut the original cover may show so use a pouffe a similar color to the yarn.

What you need

- size US 13 (9mm) circular needles
- cable needle
- Patons Wool Blend Aran (*we used 8 balls of color 88*)
- 3 large snaps

What you do

Cast on 62 sts using 3 strands of the yarn at once.

Row 1 purl

Row 2 purl

Row 3 sl1 wyib k1 (k1 yo k4) x12 (74 sts)

We worked the yo with a twist—if you work without you will get lace holes (see page 136).

Row 4–38 even rows sl1 wyif, purl to end

Row 5 sl1 wyib k1 (k5 yo k1) x12 (86 sts)

Row 7 sl1 wyib k1 (k1 yo k6) x12 (98 sts)

Row 9 sl1 wyib k1 (k7 yo k1) x12 (110 sts)

Row 11 sl1 wyib k1 (k1 yo k8) x12 (122 sts)

Row 13 sl1 wyib k1 (k9 yo k1) x12 (134 sts)

Row 15 sl1 wyib k1 (k1 yo k10) x12 (148 sts)

Row 17 sl1 wyib k1 (k11 yo k1) x12 (158 sts)

Row 19 sl1 wyib k1 (k1 yo k12) x12 (170 sts)

Row 21 bind off 2 sts purlwise, knit to end (168 sts)

Rows 23, 25 sl1 wyib knit to end

Rows 27, 29, 31, 33 sl1 wyib (k2 p3) x33, k2

Row 35 sl1 wyib (KB k2) x41, KB k1

Row 37 sl1 wyib (k1 KB k1) x41, k3

Row 39 sl1 wyib (k2 KB) x41, k3

Row 40 sl1 wyif (p2 PB) x41, p3

Rows 41, 43, 45 sl1 wyib knit to end

Row 42 sl1 wyif p1 (p2 PB) x41, p2

Row 44 sl1 wyif (PB p2) x41, PB, p1

Rows 45, 47, 49, 51, 53 sl1 wyib knit to end

Rows 46, 48, 50, 52 sl1 wyif p1 (k3 p2) x33, p1

Row 53 sl1 wyib yo knit to last st yo k1 (170 sts)

Rows 54–72 even rows sl1 wyif purl to end

Row 55 sl1 wyib [(sl2 to cn, hold in front, k2, k2 from cn; this is called 4st Cable Front) k4 k2tog k4]

x12, k1 (158 sts)

Row 57 sl1 wyib (k8 k2tog k3) x12, k1 (146 sts)

Row 59 sl1 wyib (4st Cable Front k3 k2tog k3) x12, k1 (134 sts)

Row 61 sl1 wyib (k7 k2tog k2) x12, k1 (122 sts)

Row 63 sl1 wyib (4st Cable Front k2 k2tog k2) x12, k1 (110 sts)

Row 65 sl1 wyib (k6 k2tog k1) x12, k1 (98 sts)

Row 67 sl1 wyib (4st Cable Front k1 k2tog k1) x12, k1 (86 sts)

Row 69 sl1 wyib (k5 k2tog) x12, k1 (74 sts)

Row 71 sl1 wyib (4st Cable Front k2tog) x12, k1 (62 sts)

Row 73 sl1 wyib purl to end

Row 74 double length p2tog (put your needle through to p2tog as normal but wind yarn around twice instead of once; work as a normal stitch on next row, which will release the long stitch)—repeat to end (31 sts)

Row 75 purl

Row 76 double length p2tog—repeat to end (16 sts)

Row 77 purl

continued on page 109

Row 78 (sl1 wyif k2tog psso) x 5, p1
Row 79 pull a long length of yarn
through 6 remaining stitches,
gather them together and sew
yarn through stitches twice more
to create a firm finish. Fold your
piece in half lengthways, right sides
together and sew the seam down
to row 22. Fold the plain strip down
to the cast on back on itself—this
is your band to sew one half of
the snaps onto. Sew the matching
halves onto the other edge.

This contemporary space has lots of
contrasting materials and textures, but by
keeping the muted colour palette simple
they work together, creating extra warmth.
Featured alongside the Pouffe are the
Geometric Cable Throw (see pages 62–65)
and the Intarsia Blanket (see pages 80–83).

COLOR CONTRAST

**We used a silver colored
pouffe under gray wool so
that the pouffe didn't show
through. However, if you
are feeling adventurous
you could use could use
this as a feature and
introduce a contrasting
color—hot pink or orange
under gray would be good.**

Although knitting is frankly pretty incredible, there are times when you might want to add something else when you've finished the knitting, or shape the knitting to create three-dimensional structure with the fabric itself. Once you're comfortable with the basic process you can start to question it and the application of knitting within your home. While clearly functional there is no reason why it can't be thought of as purely decorative, acting almost as a piece of art in its own right – or at the opposite end of the scale as tough and practical, such as the Ridge Rug (see pages 120–23). There really are very few limits and hopefully this chapter will help show you what can be possible with a bit of imagination.

ADDING EMBELLISHMENTS AND EXTRA TEXTURE

An old favorite and one of the easiest embellishments is adding fringe—you fold a piece of yarn in half and thread the fold from front to back through the edge then pull the free ends through the fold. Basically that's it. If you want a lot the same size, wrap your fringe yarn around a book or something similar that is the right width for the fringe you want—just cut along one edge and you're all done. If you want them all the same length you'll invariably need to give it a haircut when you've finished the fringe, or you could intentionally leave them all different lengths. We use a lot of fringe, which I'm sure you can see throughout the book— each example perfect for that specific project.

seascape wall hanging

This is one of my favorite pieces in this book—there is something very reassuring about its presence. In terms of knitting it's not difficult, but it will take a long time and some very tough, long circular needles. However, as I'm sure you'll agree the structure that is formed has so much movement and life that it really does present this ancient craft in a new light.

What you need

- 7mm circular needles (no exact US equivalent: between US sizes 10.5 and 11 needles). Adjust needle size if necessary to obtain the correct gauge.
- about 4½ pounds (2000 grams) of yarn (*we used up all sorts of yarns of a chunky weight or knitted with 2 or 3 balls of finer weight yarn together*)
- a piece of wooden dowel 48" (1.2m) long x 1" (2.5cm) diameter

What you do

The repeat is 6 sts wide and varies in length as you continue through the piece. Color changes are up to you, but to get a similar look to ours alter the color gradually. When changing to a new color do part of a row then reintroduce the last yarn occasionally; you'll avoid blocks of color, which will make the piece lose its organic feel. Of course you could just use one color throughout, which will give a much cleaner feel to the whole thing.

Cast on 120 sts

Rows 1 and 2 purl

Row 3 knit

Row 4 purl

Row 5 sl1 wyib KB ([insert your right needle under the yarn that joins the stitches on either needle and pick it up so it looks like a yo; this is called pick up] k1 KB k1 KB) x19, pick up k1 KB (140 sts)

Row 6 sl1 wyif PB (p2 PB p1 PB) x19, p2 PB

Row 7 sl1 wyib KB (yo k1 yo k1 KB k1 KB) x19, yo k1 yo k1 KB (180 sts)

Row 8 sl1 wyif PB (p4 PB p1 PB) x19, p4 PB

Row 9 sl1 wyib KB (yo k3 yo k1 KB k1 KB) x19, yo k3 yo k1 KB (220 sts)

Rows 10, 12, 14 repeat Row 8, working 2 additional purl sts each row, in place of p4

Row 11 sl1 wyib KB (yo k5 yo k1 KB k1 KB) x19, yo k5 yo k1 KB (260 sts)

Row 13 sl1 wyib KB (yo k7 yo k1 KB k1 KB) x19, yo k7 yo k1 KB (300 sts)

Row 15 sl1 wyib KB (k3 [sl1 wyib k2tog psso; this is called sk2p] k4 KB pick up k1 KB) x19, k3 sk2p k4 KB (279 sts)

Row 16 sl1 wyif PB (p8 PB p2 PB) x19, p8 PB

Row 17 sl1 wyib KB (k2 sk2p k3 KB yo k1 yo k1 KB) x19, k2 sk2p k3 KB (277 sts)

Row 18 sl1 wyif PB (p6, PB, p4, PB) x19, p6, PB

continued on page 114

CREATING TEXTURE WITHIN THE STRUCTURE OF THE KNIT ITSELF

There are two ways of creating texture, on a small scale through the use of different yarns or stitches, or on a big scale through building shape into the structure. By excessively increasing or decreasing in specific areas you will blow out or suck in the structure and can create all kinds of striking effects. The whole theory is very unpredictable though and depends enormously on exactly what you do—it's a perfect chance to really explore how yarn and stitch behave and affect each other.

Row 19 sl1 wyib KB (k1 sk2p k2 KB yo k3 yo k1 KB) x19, k1 sk2p k2 KB (275 sts)

Row 20 sl1 wyif PB (p4, PB, p6, PB) x19, p4, PB

Row 21 sl1 wyib KB (sk2p k1 KB yo k5 yo k1 KB) x19, sk2p k1 KB (273 sts)

Row 22 sl1 wyif PB (p2tog PB p8 PB) x19, p2tog PB (253 sts)

Row 23 sl1 wyib KB (k1 KB yo k7 yo k1 KB) x19, k1 KB (291 sts)

Row 24 sl1 wyif PB (p1 PB p10 PB) x19, p1 PB

Row 25 sl1 wyib KB (k1 KB yo k9 yo k1 KB) x19, k1 KB (329 sts)

Row 26 sl1 wyif PB (p1 PB p12 PB) x19, p1 PB

Row 27 sl1 wyib KB (pick up k1 KB k4 sk2p k5 KB) x19, pick up k1 KB (311 sts)

Row 28 sl1 wyif PB (p2 PB p10 PB) x19, p2 PB

Row 29 sl1 wyib KB (yo k1 yo k1 KB k3 sk2p k4 KB) x19, yo k1 yo k1 KB (313 sts)

Row 30 sl1 wyif PB (p4 PB p8 PB) x19, p4 PB

Row 31 sl1 wyib KB (yo k3 yo k1 KB k2 sk2p k3 KB) x19, yo k3 yo k1 KB (315 sts)

Row 32 sl1 wyif PB (p6 PB) x39

Row 33 sl1 wyib KB (yo k5 yo k1 KB k1 sk2p k2 KB) x19, yo k5 yo k1 KB (317 sts)

Row 34 sl1 wyif PB (p8 PB p4 PB) x19, p8 PB

Row 35 sl1 wyib KB (yo k7 yo k1 KB sk2p k1 KB) x19, yo k7 yo k1 KB (319 sts)

Row 36 sl1 wyif PB (p10 PB p2tog PB) x19, p10 PB (300 sts)

Row 37 sl1 wyib KB (yo k9 yo k1 KB k1 KB) x19, yo k9 yo k1 KB (340 sts)

Row 38 sl1 wyif PB (p12 PB p1 PB) x19, p12 PB

Row 39 sl1 wyib KB (yo k11 yo k1 KB k1 KB) x19, yo k11 yo k1 KB (380 sts)

Row 40 sl1 wyif PB (p14 PB p1 PB) x19, p14 PB

Row 41 sl1 wyib KB (k5 sk2p k6 KB k1 KB) x19, k5 sk2p k6 KB (340 sts)

Row 42 as Row 38

Row 43 sl1 wyib KB (k4 sk2p k5 KB k1 KB) x19, k4 sk2p k5 KB (300 sts)

Row 44 sl1 wyif PB (p10 PB p1 PB) x19, p10 PB

Row 45 sl1 wyib KB (k3 sk2p k4 KB pick up k1 KB) x19, k3 sk2p k4 KB (279 sts)

Row 46 sl1 wyif PB (p8 PB yo p1 yo p1 PB) x19, p8 PB (317 sts)

Row 47 sl1 wyib KB (k2 sk2p k3 KB yo k3 yo k1 KB) x19, k2 sk2p k3 KB (315 sts)

Rows 48, 50 repeat Row 46 purling 2 less sts between PBs and purling 4 additional sts between yos each row (38 sts increased each row)

Rows 49, 51 repeat Row 47 knitting 1 less st each side of sk2p and 4 additional sts between yos each row (2 sts decreased each row; 387 sts after Row 51)

Row 52 sl1 wyif PB (p2tog PB yo p13 yo p1 PB) x19, p2tog PB (405 sts)

Row 53 sl1 wyib KB (k1 KB yo k15 yo k1 KB) x19, k1 KB (443 sts)

Row 54 sl1 wyif PB (p1 PB yo p17 yo p1 PB) x19, p1 PB (481 sts)

Row 55 sl1 wyib KB (k1 KB yo k19 yo k1 KB) x19, k1 KB (519 sts)

Row 56 sl1 wyif PB (p1 PB yo p21 yo p1 PB) x19, p1 PB (557 sts)

Row 57 sl1 wyib KB (k1 KB k10 sk2p k11 KB) x19, k1 KB (519 sts)

Row 58 sl1 wyif PB (p1 PB p22 PB) x 19 p1 PB

Rows 59, 61, 63, 65 repeat Row 57 knitting 1 less st each side of sk2p each row (38 sts decreased each row; 367 sts after Row 65)

Rows 60, 62, 64, 66 repeat Row 58, working 2 fewer purl sts each row, in place of p22

Row 67 sl1 wyib KB (pick up the yarn between the stitches in the row below and knit it, making sure there is a twist in the yarn k1 KB k5 sk2p k6 KB) x19, pick up as before k1 KB (349 sts)

Row 68 sl1 wyif PB (yo p1 yo p1 PB p12 PB) x19, yo p1 yo p1 PB (389 sts)

Row 69 sl1 wyib KB (yo k3 yo k1 KB k4 sk2p k5 KB) x19, yo k3 yo k1 KB (391 sts)

Rows 70, 72, 74, 76 repeat Row 68 purling 2 less sts between PBs and an additional 4 sts between yos each row (40 sts increased each row)

Rows 71, 73, 75, 77 repeat Row 69 knitting 1 less st each side of sk2p and 4 additional sts between yos each row (2 sts increased each row; 559 sts after Row 77)

Row 78 sl1 wyif PB (yo p21 yo p1 PB p2tog PB) x19, yo p21 yo p1 PB (580 sts)

Row 79 sl1 wyib KB (yo k23 yo k1 KB k1 KB) x19, yo k23 yo k1 KB (620 sts)

Row 80 sl1 wyif PB (p26 PB p1 PB) x19, p26 PB

Row 81 sl1 wyib KB (k11 sk2p k12 KB k1 KB) x19, k11 sk2p k12 KB (580 sts)

Rows 82, 84, 86, 88, 90, 92 repeat Row 80, working 2 fewer purl sts each row, in place of p26

Rows 83, 85, 87, 89, 91 repeat Row 81 knitting 1 less st each side of sk2p each row (40 sts decreased each row; 380 sts after Row 91)

Row 93 sl1 wyib KB (k5 sk2p k6 KB pick up k1 KB) x19, k5 sk2p k6 KB (359 sts)

Row 94 sl1 wyif PB (p12 PB yo p1 yo p1 PB) x19, p12 PB (397 sts)

Row 95 sl1 wyib KB (k4 sk2p k5 KB yo k3 yo k1 KB) x19, k4 sk2p k5 KB (395 sts)

Rows 96, 98, 100, 102 repeat Row 94 purling 2 less sts between PBs and 4 additional sts between yos each row (38 sts increased each row)

Rows 97, 99, 101, 103 repeat Row 95 knitting 1 less st each side of sk2p and 4 additional sts between yos each row (2 sts decreased each row; 539 sts after Row 103)

Row 104 sl1 wyif PB (p2tog PB yo p21 yo p1 PB) x19, p2tog PB (557 sts)

Row 105 sl1 wyib KB (k1 KB yo k23 yo k1 KB) x19, k1 KB (595 sts)

Row 106 sl1 wyif PB (p1 PB yo p25 yo p1 PB) x19, p1 PB (633 sts)

Row 107 sl1 wyib KB (k1 KB yo k27 yo k1 KB) x19, k1 KB (671 sts)

Row 108 sl1 wyif PB (p1 PB yo p29 yo p1 PB) x19, p1 PB 709 sts)

Row 109 sl1 wyib KB (k1 KB k14 sk2p k15 KB) x19, k1 KB (671 sts)

Row 110 sl1 wyif PB (p1 PB p30, PB) x19, p1 PB

Rows 111, 113, 115, 117, 119, 121, 123, 125 repeat Row 109 knitting 1 less st each side of sk2p each row (38 sts decreased each row; 367 sts after Row 125)

Rows 112, 114, 116, 118, 120, 122, 124, 126 repeat Row 110 purling 2 less sts each row in place of p30

Repeat Rows 67–103 (or if you want to make your hanging longer Rows 67–126 is a full repeat)
Bind off knitwise.

Fold the top edge over the dowel and sew in place.

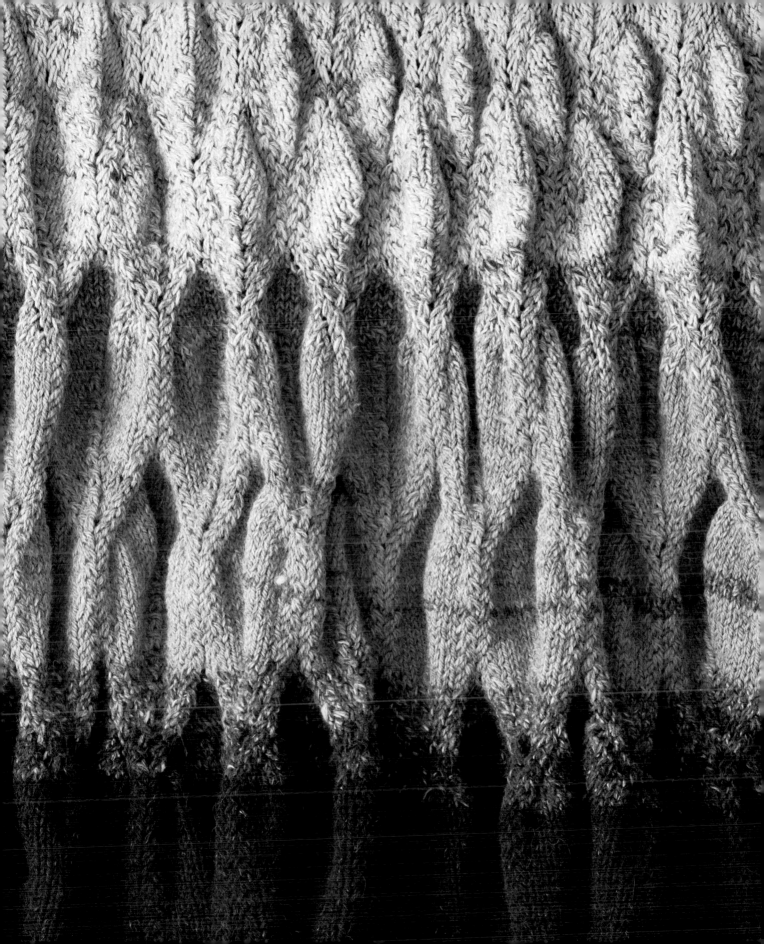

Weaving

You can weave anything that will fit into any part of your knitting, but to make it look more considered think about what you want to do before you start knitting and you can create gaps where you want to weave later. Ideal stitches for this are lace holes and double length stitches (see page 47), but you can also just do a row with a finer yarn and weave into that, or go under the gap created by cables.

Gathering

You can create gathers in several ways: either weave a separate piece of yarn or ribbon through a line of holes and pull it to gather it up, or you can knit it into the actual structure by using specific stitches.

When you've got to grips with a few different types of stitches you'll notice that even with the same amount of stitches and rows some stitches make the knitting dramatically tighter or looser. The most extreme example of this that I've included in this book are the basket stitch on page 47 (which really pulls in) and the double length stitch on page 47 (this is super loose). Generally speaking, if you measure your gauge for both techniques there will be a bigger difference between either the stitch or row gauges—pick the one that has the bigger difference and alternate in the opposite direction. For instance, if there is a big difference between the stitch gauges do a good few rows of one, then do some of the other. Alternate like this and the technique with fewer stitches/inch will start to gather up. For a bigger repeat/inch difference you will need to alternate between the techniques across the rows.

Another method to gather is used in the ridge rug (see pages 120–123) and chair cushion covers (see pages 98–101) in which you do a few rows then hook up the stitches from a row several below so that the ones in between gather up.

ridge rug

This rug is entirely adaptable to whatever size you need, it's wonderfully springy and if you use some tough yarn it will be fairly hard-wearing too. The pattern is easy to add stripes into and simple to do once you've got the hang of it. Ours is pretty uncomplicated and looks really chic as a result.

What you need

• size US 13 (9mm) needles
• Patons Wool Blend Aran (*We held 2 ends of each color together and used two colors: 13 balls of shade 10 dark brown for the main color [Col A] and 7 balls of shade 14 marled brown [Col B]).*

What you do

The stitch gauge for our rug is 2½ sts/in and 8 rows (1 repeat)/¾" (2 cm). Our rug was 87 sts wide [34¾" (88.5cm)] x70 8-row repeats. [52½" (133.5c=m)]

Cast on using however many stitches you need for the size of rug you want using two balls of Col A

Row 1 purl (Col A)
Row 2 purl (Col A)
Row 3 knit (Col B)
Row 4 purl (Col B)
Row 5 knit (Col B)
Row 6 knit (Col A)
Row 7 purl (Col A)
Row 8 knit (Col A)
Row 9 purl (Col A)
Row 10 Using Col B look at the front of your piece and using the right needle hook the Col B purled stitch a few rows directly below the next stitch up onto the left needle, then purl this and the original first stitch together. Repeat this all along the row.

Rows 3–10 is one repeat so just do as many as you need.

To finish using Col A do one row purl then bind off knitwise.

The squishy ridges
this rug is made up
of provide an inviting
contrast of warmth
against the polished
concrete floor.

woven wall hanging

This is a deceptively simple design that uses a lot of weaving. We used a selection of yarns that are off-white in color but you could substitute any yarns of approximately the same weight as the ones we used.

What you need
- size US 15 (10mm) circular needles
- Rowan Big Wool (4 balls)
- Debbie Bliss Rialto Chunky (3 balls)
- Debbie Bliss Donegal Luxury Tweed Chunky (1 ball)
- Debbie Bliss Amalfi (paler color x 4, darker color x 3)
- Rowan British Sheep Breeds DK (2 balls)
- willow sticks 59" (150cm) long
- flat paper tape ¼" (4mm) x 16½ yards (15m)
- 2 pieces of wooden dowel 1 yard (100cm) long painted the same color/s as the first and last 8 rows

What you do
Cast on 101 sts using the Big Wool

Rows 1–10 knit odd rows, purl even rows

Row 11 k7, introduce 1 end of paler Amalfi with 1 of Rialto and p87, take another ball of Big Wool and k7

Row 12 Throughout this pattern always follow the yarn layout in the row below until instructed otherwise. Change between yarns using the intarsia method as described on page 140. p7 double length purl (put your needle through to purl as normal but wind yarn around twice instead of once; work as a normal stitch on next row, which will release the long stitch) x87, p7

Row 13 k7 turn your piece p7 turn again k7 p87 k7 turn piece p7 turn piece k7 (These extra 'edge only' rows allow space for the long stitches to fit.)

Row 14–27 repeat Rows 12–13

Row 28 purl using Big Wool across the whole row

Row 29 k7, introduce Donegal p87, using separate ball Big Wool k7

Row 30 p7 k87 p7

Rows 31–34 repeat Rows 29–30

Row 35 as Row 29

Row 36 as Row 28

Row 37 k7 p87 k7

Row 38 p7 double purl x87, p7

Row 39 k7 turn piece p7 turn again k7 p87 k7 turn piece p7 turn piece k7

Rows 40–49 repeat Rows 38–39

Row 50 purl

Row 51 knit

Row 52 purl

Row 53 k7, introduce Donegal p87, introduce separate ball Big Wool k7

Row 54 p7 k87 p7

Row 55 knit using Big Wool

Row 56 purl

Rows 57–64 repeat Rows 55–56

Row 65 k7 p87 k7

Row 66 p7, taking 2 ends of paler Amalfi and 1 of Rowan DK p87, taking a new ball of Big Wool p7

Row 67 k7 k87 k7

Row 68 p7, introduce 3 ends of darker Amalfi k87, using the Big Wool as in row below p7

Row 69 k7 k1 (yo k2tog) x43, k7

Rows 70–79 repeat Rows 66–67

Rows 80–139 repeat Rows 68–79

Rows 140–143 repeat Rows 68–71

Row 144 purl using Big Wool

Row 145 knit

Rows 146–151 repeat Rows 44–145

Bind off knitwise

Steam the hanging (see page 140), wrap the dowels in the first and last 8 rows and sew them in. Add loops and hang it while you weave the willow and paper strips horizontally and vertically into the various gaps.

WOVEN WALL HANGING 125

Here you can see the detail of the paper and willow woven in the knitted holes. You can intentionally add lace holes to anything with a view to weaving them later—it's a simple but effective technique.

Knitting is exactly like baking; there are a few ingredients that can be combined in a million different ways to create endless possibilities. This section covers the step by step of how each knitting "ingredient" is made to help you on your way. Although basic knitting and purling are simple to do you'd be surprised at how many small variations there are, each having a slightly different effect on the overall piece. Because hand knitting is passed from person to person, each of us assumes we all do it the same, but I've worked with so many knitters over the years that I now know if you gave 50 people the same yarn and pattern, you'd get 50 slightly different items back!

THE ESSENTIALS

I have included here step by step instructions for how I personally do everything, plus some other popular techniques. My knit stitches in particular are different from those of a lot of other people and there are subtle differences in some of the other techniques too. I was taught to knit like this and find it a simple method. It's especially good as it creates quite a loose fabric, the stitches of which are easier to play around with and manipulate (when you've got the hang of the basics) and want to push the technique further.

If you can already knit in your own way then the majority of the patterns here will work out just fine, however some of the ones that involve working the stitches in a particular way (keep an eye open for baskets, extra long stitches, and yos in particular) may need you to refer to my method if yours isn't quite the same, or if the pattern isn't doing what you expected! Everyone is individual, so do whatever works best for you. Hopefully this book has inspired you to realize there is no "right" way and by exploring different options you may discover something new along the way.

abbreviations

k knit

p purl

st/s stitch/es

k2tog/p2tog knit 2 stitches together/purl two stitches together

sl slip
Often the first stitch in a row is slipped to give a good edge, especially if it's going to be a raw edge and not sewn into a seam, such as on a blanket

wyib/wyif with yarn in back/ with yarn in front.

psso pass the slip stitch over

yo yarn over

KB/PB knit basket/purl basket. To make these you basically work the second stitch first, then the first and slip both off together. This only works if you knit and purl as I do, so check my instructions. When knitting, go behind the work to get to the second stitch, for purling go in front.

st/in stitches per inch, or the gauge

r/in rows per inch

cn is a double pointed needle used for making cables. Some people like them — some don't, I've written both methods for you (see Cables page 137)

DK double knit (weight of yarn)

casting on

Knit-on cast on
There are many ways to cast on—this is the way I do it.

Put your needles together and tie the yarn around them. Cross your needles so the right is behind the left (1). Hold the left needle like a spoon along with the short tail end of the yarn. Use your left

forefinger and thumb to hold the cross in the needles while your right hand takes the yarn behind and then back between the needles (2). Keep your left hand firm and holding the yarn and needle in your right hand keep the yarn taut. Move the right needle back through the loop towards you, bringing the yarn wrapped around it through the loop too (3, 4). Using your right needle, place this new loop back on the left needle. Do this so the right needle is behind the left and ready to make the next stitch (5). Repeat this for as many stitches as you need.

Long tail cast on

This method is also known as Continental cast on or double cast on. Place a slip loop on the right needle, with a tail three times the width of your cast on. Hold the ball and tail ends in the left hand and wrap the tail end round the thumb (1). Lift the ball end with your forefinger and insert the tip of the needle into the strand at the front of the thumb and through the strand on the forefinger from top to bottom (2). Bring the strand on the forefinger through the strand on the thumb to make a stitch (3).

Single thumb cast on

Also known as backward loop, provisional or twisted loop cast on, this uses a single needle. Place a slip loop on the right needle—this is your first stitch. Close the fingers of the left hand over the yarn, with the end attached to the needle held between thumb and forefinger. Move the thumb from left to right under the needle end of the yarn and wrap it around the thumb. Insert the needle through the strand on the thumb and transfer the loop to the needle. Tighten and continue.

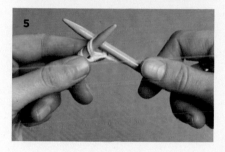

Above: Long tail cast on
Below: Single thumb cast on

knit

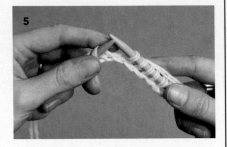

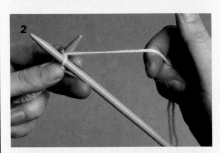

There are many ways to knit, this is how I do it (some people call this "through back loop") and all the instructions in this book that include "knit" refer to this method. I use it all the time as it is how I learned and I find working the stitches like this allows me to manipulate them more easily.

My knit is basically the same as my cast on, except instead of placing the loop you've pulled through (1) back on the left needle, you use it to pull the stitch it came through off the left needle (2). This is one stitch knitted. You can then move onto the next (3) and continue until you've knitted all the stitches you want (4, 5).

purl

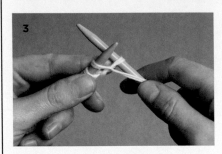

To purl I insert the right needle from right to left through the stitch, crossing this needle in front of the left (1). Bring the yarn toward you and then back between the needles (2). Use your right needle to pull the loop through (3) and use it to pull the stitch it came through off the left

bind off

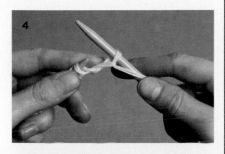

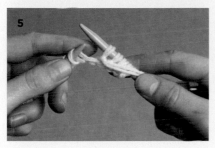

needle (4). Continue for as many purls as you need (5).

You may notice that my knits and purls are exact opposites of each other—they are easy to learn and then play around with when you're more confident. The instructions through this book assume you knit and purl like this, so if it doesn't look like you expect check your technique against mine.

There are two ways to bind off: knitwise and purlwise. Binding off is easy—you simply knit/purl 2 stitches and use your left needle to pull the first over the second and off the needle. You then knit/purl another stitch and pull the previous over that, continuing for as many as you want to bind off. Knitwise will make the bound off chain on the side facing you, purlwise will put the chain on the back.

slip

slip

To slip a stitch simply transfer it from the left needle to the right without working it (1, 2). With yarn in back (wyib) indicates you bring the yarn to the back of the work (if it's not already there) before slipping the stitch, with yarn in front (wyif) means taking the yarn to the front (3, 4). When you've slipped the stitch you'll need to take the yarn back to the side you need it on to continue your row.

psso

psso stands for "pass the slipped stitch over" and is commonly used to decrease when used with slipped stitches (see Seascape wall hanging pages 112–17). The same method is used for all sorts of things (notably binding off). You use your left needle to hook the second stitch over the first (1) and off (2, 3) from the right needle.

psso

k2tog

k2tog

To "knit 2 together" simply go through 2 st instead of one (1), pull the loop through as normal (2, 3), and pull both stitches you went through off together (4).

p2tog

To "purl 2 together" simply go through 2 stitches instead of one (1), pull the loop through as normal (2, 3), and pull both stitches you went through off together (4).

p2tog

yo

To make a yarn over (yo) is simple: hold the needles apart with your left hand (1), take the yarn over the right needle (2—on a purl row bring the yarn back over the needle and towards you between the two) and work the next stitch as normal (3). When you go back across this yo on the following row there are two ways you can work this stitch—with or without a twist. With a twist will close the hole so you have just neatly created a new stitch—when you get to the yo push it forwards (4) and work it as normal (5) according to the stitches before and after it (shown here is a purl row so I've worked it like a purl). When you slip it off the new stitch will have a twist in it.

To create a new stitch and a lace hole work your yo without a twist, and work the yo through the opposite side of the stitch from normal (6, 7). When you slip the new stitch off it will have no twist, creating a hole below it (8).

If you're making a yo between a knit and purl stitch you'll need to work out which method to do to create what you want.

cable

Decide how many stitches wide you want your cable and where it will be in the row. To make your cable slip half its stitches onto a cn (1). Hold this in the front (2) or back of the work (this alters the direction of the cable). Work the second half of the cable (3, 4) then work the first half from the cn (5, 6). This is a complete cable—the standard is to do this once per the same number of rows as the cable is wide in stitches (so 8st wide would be cabled every 8 rows) but you can change this if you want.

When you get the hang of it you can forget the cn— just slide the first half of stitches off (hanging in mid-air on the side of the knitting you want them and keeping your needles close together to avoid dropping these), slip the second half onto the right needle, pick up the first half on the left needle, and slip the second half back onto the left too. Then you can work them all in one go. It sounds complicated, but it isn't.

The theory of repeats

For the patterns in this book a repeat sequence of stitches in a row is included in (round brackets) or for more complex sequences that require repeats within repeats in [square brackets] and this indicates the section to be repeated. Sometimes a specific number of repeats is required which will be indicated — otherwise just keep going while you have enough stitches to do so.

Button holes

Knit indicated number of stitches. Bring the yarn to the front. Slip 1 stitch from the left needle to the right and take the yarn to the back. Drop it there.

Slip another stitch from the left to the right then pass the last slipped stitch over it — a bit like binding off. Keep binding off stitches like this until you have done the correct number for your button hole width. Slip the last bound off stitch back to the left needle and turn the piece round so you are facing the other side.

Pick up the yarn you dropped and cast on as many new stitches as you bound off. Then cast on one more but before you put the new stitch on the left needle bring the yarn towards you between the previous stitches and this one.

Turn the work round again.

Slip 1 stitch from the left to the right and pass the last new one over it. Pull your yarn to make sure the buttonhole is firm then continue your row.

Working out stitch gauge

Your stitch gauge is simply the amount of stitches and rows you personally create per inch when using a certain pair of needles and yarn. Yarn companies give

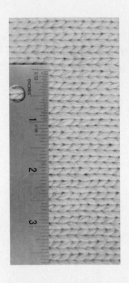
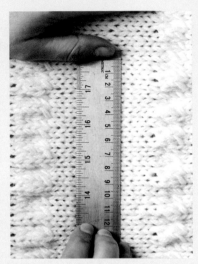

an indication of what you can expect this to be but actually everyone is different. In order to be able to design whatever you want, and use whatever needle/yarn combination you like, the ability to figure this out is very useful!

When you have discovered a particular knit you like you can work out the stitch gauge or stitches per inch (st/in) by dividing the number of stitches counted by the number of inches covered. For example 14 stitches over 4in = 3½ stitches per in. Measure your stitches like this in groups — don't ever try to measure individual stitches. To work out the row gauge measure a group of rows and do exactly the same calculation. Make sure you follow the same stitch along the rows or it won't be accurate. This sample needs to be about 20 to 30 stitches wide depending on how big the stitches are (more are required for small stitches). Don't measure stitches nearer the edge where the gauge will be less consistent. To make this easier put your sample or swatch on a flat surface and use a ruler to squash the piece so you can count the stitches/rows easily at the natural gauge without it moving around. Be precise with your measurements— on big pieces especially it does matter.

Then when you decide you want to make something in that stitch/yarn/needle combination simply multiply the width and height by your gauge and you'll know how many stitches and rows you need. If your pattern has a repeat you need to check the repeat fits into the number of stitches you need.

Sewing up

The first thing to do is to sew up any seams. To do this place the two pieces you want to sew with their wrong sides together. Use safety pins to hold the pieces together, matching up any points you want to be together. When you bind off you should leave nice long tails of yarn attached to the knitting so you can use these to sew up the seams. Ideally you work from one point to another using a neat overstitch. Make sure you use a nice big, blunt darning needle and go through stitches— do not split the yarn with your stitches. Use the yarn you knitted with to sew, so your stitches will end up invisible.

If your yarn starts to run out do 2 stitches in one place and sew the yarn back down under the stitches you just made. If you need more yarn introduce it by going through these stitches and popping out where you just finished. Always leave about 1/4–3/4" (1–2cm) of yarn (depending on the size of the item) sticking out on the inside— when you wash it fill felt the end in and shut the seam from unravelling. When you open your piece out, the seam should sit totally flat and the stitches should disappear into the knit.

How to sew up a pillow cover

Take all three pieces of your cover and line them up making sure all your cast on edges and bound off edges are in a long line. Also make sure the button holes are on the outside edge of the line.

Pin the pieces together (right sides together) and sew down the seams so you have one long piece. Lay this flat, right side up.

Fold the overlap (with button hole) so the seam is on the edge and the button hole edge is half way across the front. Pin this together at the top and bottom. Then work out the difference in stitch number between the underlay and overlap, fold the underlay over so the seam is on the edge and it crosses the overlap by this number of stitches. Pin this in place and sew along the top and bottom (through 2 layers on each side and 3 layers in the middle). Turn this the right way out and you'll find you've made an envelope style cover. Put the pad in and sew on the button so you've a good snug fit.

It'll come out in the wash . . .

Knitting can have very different qualities pre- and post-wash — often a bouncy structure can become a wonderful loose drape and visa versa. So unless you plan on never washing what you're making, it's a good idea to give small knitted samples a wash to see how they will look in the long run rather than assuming they will stay the same. To wash your piece have a look at the instructions on the yarn label. The main things guaranteed to ruin knitting are hot water and a fast, long spin cycle. We always wash our knits in lukewarm water with a mild detergent, rinse them out then put them in to spin on a short slow cycle. We then lie them flat to dry on an airer — not on direct heat. The bigger the piece the more important it is to support the weight as it dries or it can easily distort the shape.

Steam

We are huge fans of steaming — a good steam will transform your wobbly edged cloth into something beautiful. You only need a regular iron with a strong steam setting. Simply put your piece flat on the ironing board in the right shape, then hover the iron over the knitting giving it as much steam as possible. Don't touch the piece with the iron; you only want the steam. Put the iron down and gently pull the piece into shape — as it cools it will set. If you need to you can repeat this until it looks perfect.

Intarsia

Adding contrasting yarns within rows to create vertical contrasting panels is called Intarsia. If your sections start at the cast on you'll need to cast on with the different yarns in their sections. Cast on the first section

then take the second yarn, tie it to the first close to the needle and cast the next section on (leaving the first yarn where the knot is). When you come to changing from one yarn to another in a row change over as follows; take the first yarn you're using to your left hand and hold it taut, then pick up the second yarn and make your next stitch taking the second over the first you're holding taught. On a purl row do this on the side of the knitting that faces you; on the knit side do it on the back. After a few rows you'll end up with a neat row of stitches where the two yarns join.

If you want to change the width of your stripe do a trial first to see what happens at the changeover. Big changes will leave you with floats, which some people don't like. They can be sewn in or cut and knotted. You could also add a backing to your piece to hide this.

Cabled footstool sketches

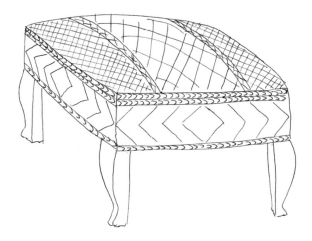

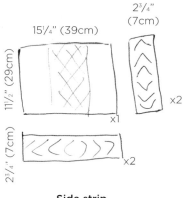

15¼" (39cm)

2¾" (7cm)

11½" (29cm)

x1

x2

2¾" (7cm)

x2

Side strip

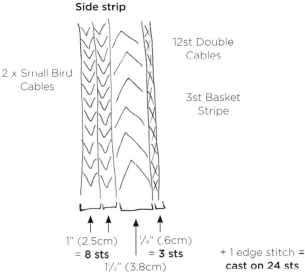

2 x Small Bird Cables

12st Double Cables

3st Basket Stripe

1" (2.5cm) = **8 sts**

1½" (3.8cm) = **12 sts**

¼" (.6cm) = **3 sts**

+ 1 edge stitch = **cast on 24 sts**

Top

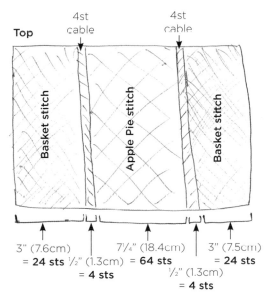

4st cable

4st cable

Basket stitch

Apple Pie stitch

Basket stitch

3" (7.6cm) = **24 sts**

½" (1.3cm) = **4 sts**

7¼" (18.4cm) = **64 sts**

½" (1.3cm) = **4 sts**

3" (7.5cm) = **24 sts**

+ 6 single stitches between each pattern = **cast on 126 sts**

Side strip length

Cable row gauge = 8¾ rows/in

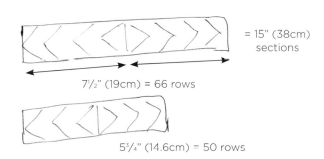

= 15" (38cm) sections

7½" (19cm) = 66 rows

5¾" (14.6cm) = 50 rows

WRITING PATTERNS

To write your own pattern you first need to do some sketches to work out the design you want. Then measure your object in panels and write down the size of each one.

You'll need to do some samples of the stitches you want using the yarn and needle size you'll use for the project. Use these to work out the stitch gauge and apply this to each part of each panel, which will show you the stitches and rows required. To write the pattern for each panel see Combining different stitch patterns on the next page. You can see in this sketch how I have worked out each section and the full pattern is on pages 94–97 where you can also see the finished project.

Combining different stitch patterns

Do a sketch of what you'd like to make — you can play around with your samples to see how the patterns look together. Start with something with a simple shape such as a pillow or a throw and then decide the size. Start to work out what area you would like to cover with each pattern across the width. Think about whether you would like some kind of detail on the edge, and include this in your working out. When you know your measurements across the width you can use these to work out how many stitches each section of pattern will need (be careful to make sure any repeats work out with this number). Then add all the stitches required together — this is your cast on number.

To work out the rows you need to work out an average between the gauges of the different patterns. If the row gauges are similar this will even them out just fine for your calculations. Multiply your desired length by this gauge and that is how many rows you need.

Be aware that If you have two patterns with vastly different row gauges as vertical stripes, the one with more rows per inch will start to create gathers in the one with less. Try not to do this to start with. (Later on though you can try this intentionally — when exploited this looks really pretty.)

When you write your pattern you need all your instructions for each row of each pattern — work across each row applying the relevant pattern to the number of stitches required. Don't forget that your drawing is seen from the right side so the written pattern will follow the different sections in order from right to left. On the back of the fabric you need to follow the pattern layout in your drawing from left to right.

Circles

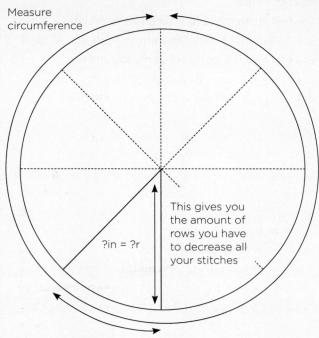

Measure circumference

This gives you the amount of rows you have to decrease all your stitches

?in = ?r

Divide circumference by number of sections ?in = ?st
This is your cast on per section

Converting shaped drawings to knit instructions

The first thing that often surprises non-knitters is that you don't need a paper pattern to work from — what you do need is a good set of measurements.

Basically you need to know how wide you want your piece to start off and then how much you need to decrease or increase, and where, over a certain distance. You convert all these measurements to stitches (all widths) and rows (all lengths).

To deal with curves you do really need to draw them as the actual size. Then you use a ruler and make your curve into a series of straight lines. Try to make it into as few as possible and then work out the width and height of each line to find out what stitches/rows are required and how much you add/take away per row.

To deal with circles is surprisingly easy. Measure all the way around your circle and then the distance to the center. Assuming you want to start at the edge and work in you now know how many stitches to start with and how many rows you have to get rid of them all. However to make it look like a circle you can't just take it off each side — you need to think of your circle like a cake with lots of pieces or little triangles. By dividing up the cast on width into sections and decreasing a bit in each one you'll end up with a circle. The more sections you have the more round it will be (only 4 sections for instance, and it will probably look more like a square).

Curves

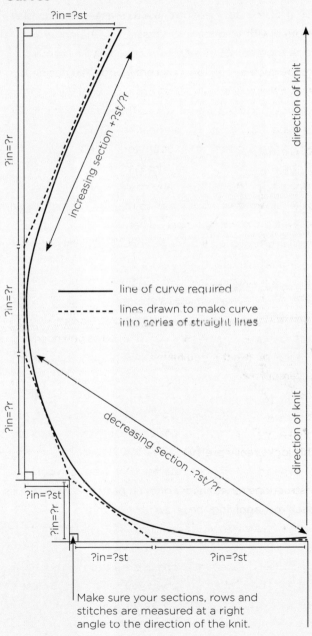

?in=?st

?in=?r

increasing section +?st/?r

?in=?r

——————— line of curve required

- - - - - - - lines drawn to make curve into series of straight lines

?in=?r

decreasing section -?st/?r

direction of knit

direction of knit

?in=?st

?in=?r

?in=?st   ?in=?st

Make sure your sections, rows and stitches are measured at a right angle to the direction of the knit.

suppliers

SOURCES FOR YARNS USED IN THIS BOOK
www.debbieblissonline.com
www.knitrowan.com
www.patonsyarns.com

SOURCES FOR RIBBON USED IN THIS BOOK
www.texere-yarns.co.uk

acknowledgments

I would like to thank every one involved in making this book happen:
My lovely, patient, and determined knitters who helped knit the samples—
thank you so much Brenda Watson, Ann McFaull, Brenda Jennings,
Joan Doyle, Pauline Dodd, Doreen Payne, Sally Cuthbert, and Brenda Willows.

Sophie for her endless sewing and organizing skills.

Debbie Bliss for her lovely yarn.

I would also like to thank all my family who are endlessly supportive no
matter how much knitting there is about the place!

All photography is by Ben Anders, apart from the image on pages 8 to 9, which is by Polly Eltes,
and the images far left on page 131 and left on page 138, which are by Ruth Cross.